PEER TUTORING FOR INDIVIDUALIZED INSTRUCTION

Peer Tutoring for Individualized Instruction

STEWART W. EHLY
University of Iowa

STEPHEN C. LARSEN
University of Texas

ALLYN AND BACON, INC.
Boston | London | Sydney | Toronto

Library of Congress Cataloging in Publication Data

Ehly, Stewart W   1949–
  Peer tutoring for individualized instruction.

  Bibliography: p.
  Includes index.
  1. Peer-group tutoring of students. 2. Tutors and tutoring. 3. Handicapped children—Education.
I. Larsen, Stephen C., 1943– joint author. II. Title.
LC41.E36   371.39'4   79-22847
ISBN 0-205-06878-2

Printed in the United States of America

To my wife, Pamela.
S. W. E.

CONTENTS

PREFACE

In preparing this volume, the authors have attempted to provide the reader with a working knowledge of peer tutoring. The audience for this book is the classroom teacher and school administrator who plan to implement peer tutoring in the classroom. Over the past several years, the authors have been approached by many teachers who have heard of the benefits of peer tutoring. While many people have discussed peer tutoring, few sources of information on the process of tutoring are available. After reviewing existing manuals and articles on peer tutoring, the authors discovered that little had been written on the methods of implementation of peer tutoring. To remedy this deficit, the authors have developed this volume.

The organization of the book was designed specifically to aid the practitioner in implementing peer tutoring. Chapters are organized to provide a background to the history of tutoring, methods for developing programs, and examples of the many forms the process can take. The chapters are organized as follows.

Chapter 1 provides a brief overview of peer tutoring in the classroom. Brief examples are presented to illustrate the structure and outcomes of typical programs using this technique.

Chapter 2 explores in depth the historical antecedents of peer tutoring, as well as more modern applications of these methods. Emphasis is given in part to large-scale programs that have been evaluated for the benefits of peer tutoring. A summary of research findings in the area is provided for the reader.

Chapter 3 examines the development of peer tutoring programs. Goals for both tutors and learners are presented. Additional consideration is given to selecting and training tutors, selecting students to be tutored, pairing tutor and learner, and models for structuring the peer tutoring process.

Chapter 4 delves into the intricacies of the structure of peer tutoring programs. Each structural consideration is highlighted so that the reader will be able to construct his/her own program. Topics include space, time, and working arrangements in the tutorial process.

Chapter 5 provides the reader with information on structuring the content of peer tutoring programs. Special attention is given to the development of materials, and to shaping these materials within the confines of the tutorial structure.

Chapters 6, 7, and 8 explore the application of the tutorial process across a variety of situations. Chapter 6 focuses on the organization of large-scale tutorial programs, providing the reader with guidelines for developing such programs within any educational system. Emphasis is given to the "selling points" of peer tutoring. Chapter 7 explores examples of existing tutorial programs with students who exhibit physical, emotional, or learning handicaps. After discussing these projects, the authors provide the reader with some choices in structuring tutorial programs for handicapped children. Chapter 8 examines in a similar fashion programs implemented with children in a variety of institutional settings. The use of adult tutors is explored also.

In writing this book, the authors have relied on their years of experience in both the development and assessment of peer tutoring programs; whenever possible, examples of existing programs are given to illustrate the reality of restraints in the typical educational environment. The authors hope that users of this book will develop their own programs with children learning successfully through peer tutoring the ultimate goal.

PEER TUTORING FOR INDIVIDUALIZED INSTRUCTION

1
AN INTRODUCTION TO PEER TUTORING

Mrs. Carter knew that she had to do something. Ronald was becoming more and more of a problem in class. He was performing below grade level in most academic areas and seemed uninterested in classroom happenings. On several occasions, Mrs. Carter, with some hesitation, felt compelled to reprimand Ronald for not paying attention in class. Mrs. Williams, the school counselor and a close friend of Mrs. Carter, was acquainted with Ronald's difficulties. She suggested to Mrs. Carter that Ronald might become more involved in the school's academic programs if he could be made to assume responsibility for teaching another child in some subject area. Ronald was near grade level in math but resisted any type of class work which involved any aspect of English. Mrs. Williams offered to schedule Ronald to work with a younger child after school on the younger child's arithmetic lessons. Ronald agreed to this and worked for thirty minutes a day, four days a week, to teach basic arithmetic skills to his partner. The teacher provided the materials used during the lessons. Ronald was responsible for correcting his partner's work. In a few weeks, Mrs. Carter noted a marked change in Ronald's academic and social behavior. Ronald was becoming more attentive in class and more willing to volunteer for general classroom activities. Ronald even offered to help other students in his class with their math assignments.

Ronald and his teacher are examples of people who have participated in peer tutoring programs. Not all peer tutoring programs are as simple to initiate as was the case with Ronald and Mrs. Carter. But most instances of peer tutoring share common elements, all of which will be fully described in this book. Obviously, the first step in becoming knowledgeable in peer tutoring techniques is to answer the question: What is peer tutoring?

PEER TUTORING: A DEFINITION

At its most basic level, peer tutoring is children teaching other children, usually on a one-to-one basis. The term "peer tutoring" has been used in the literature to describe situations in which a person provides instructional assistance and guidance to another person (Cohen, Kirk and Dickson, 1972). Readers of this book will be more concerned with those instances in which children tutor other children. Studies of peer tutoring often have reported on older students teaching some subject to younger students, a situation more accurately labeled cross-age tutoring. However, unless specified otherwise, the term "peer tutoring" will be used to describe both cross- and same-age tutoring arrangements.

The process of peer tutoring is certainly not a new concept. Children have been helping and teaching each other for as long as people have banded together with common goals. The literature in anthropology mentions many societies which expect or demand the transmission of information and skill from older to younger children. More familiarly, early settlers in America had to rely on the more mature of their children to handle homemaking and caretaking chores and to teach these tasks to younger siblings, while the parents attended to matters outside of the household. When schooling became possible on a community level, children were sent to one-room schoolhouses to receive their instruction. With one teacher to provide that instruction, older or more able students were given the responsibility of teaching younger or less gifted students on a part-time basis. The tutoring arrangements apparently worked. Children were able to learn their lessons even in a multi-grade classroom with only one teacher.

Modern day equivalents of earlier tutoring arrangements have been developed to ensure that greater attention is given to the needs of each student. Consequently, more time is made available to the teacher to work with students needing special attention. The teacher can make maximum use of the additional time to develop lesson plans or to meet with support staff regarding special problems and needs.

An abundance of studies, mostly anecdotal in nature, has been published on conducting peer tutoring programs in the schools. The anecdotal studies have been very positive in their descriptions of the success of such programs. In the chapters which follow, emphasis will be placed primarily on how tutoring programs may be established in individual schools. Step by step the authors will present guidelines for the best utilization of teacher and student time and energy in a tutoring program. Various empirical and anecdotal studies will be examined to clarify the advantages and limitations of the various forms of tutoring programs.

HOW PEER TUTORING CAN WORK IN THE SCHOOL

Many examples of tutoring programs are available from even a cursory review of the literature of education and psychology. These examples include programs that employed students of varying ages, grade levels, sexes, ethnic identities, academic and intellectual potentials. Programs have succeeded with students of every characteristic. Listed below are some examples of tutorial arrangements that have met the needs of teachers and students.

The first case is an example from an elementary school that used a peer tutorial arrangement to meet the needs of a student. The tutorial objectives for this student were specified as a sequence of individual learning steps. This example illustrates some basic components of every tutoring program: the one-to-one relationship, the creation of learning and behavioral objectives, and the structuring of materials.

Billy was a second-grade child who had experienced great difficulty in mastering basic reading skills. His failure had reached the point where he was beginning to withdraw when in the class and to come into conflict with his peers in the classroom and on the playground. His teacher, Miss Jackson, was convinced that Billy could learn if given some intensive one-to-one remediation. She felt that while she had time to devote to this task after school, singling Billy out from his peers would only serve to reinforce feelings of failure. In addition, the after-school work would place her in the difficult role of a potential disciplinarian which could interfere with her other interactions with Billy.

As an alternative action, Miss Jackson called upon one of her former students. James had been a student in Miss Jackson's room two years ago, and while not being an outstanding student academically, he always had seemed to be sensitive to the problems of his classmates. Miss Jackson first explained the tutoring idea to James and his teacher, and obtained their permission for James to participate. Miss Jackson arranged for three twenty-minute sessions per week during which Billy would be presented lessons in reading. After carefully reviewing Billy's academic weaknesses in reading, Miss Jackson specified an instructional objective as well as several subobjectives related to that objective for Billy. Once she was sure that James understood the steps of the instructional sequence, the program was initiated. Her instructional objective for Billy was as follows:

Instructional objective—To identify the initial consonants of words.
Subskills (to be emphasized by the tutor):
Step 1. Billy should be able to listen to the tutor as he pronounces words which have a specific initial consonant.
Step 2. Billy should be able to clap his hands each time that he hears a word that starts with a selected initial consonant as the tutor pronounces a group of words.
Step 3. Billy should be able to put an X on the picture which begins with a selected initial consonant when he is given a choice of two stimulus pictures.
Step 4. Billy should be able to sort a group of pictures according to a specific initial consonant whenever he is given a group of pictures differing in initial consonants of the pictured word.
Step 5. Billy should be able to say words that begin with a particular initial consonant.

At the conclusion of two weeks (a total of six sessions), Billy demonstrated mastery of the given subskills and attainment of the instructional goal. Miss Jackson continued to sequence additional skills and encouraged James to continue the warm supportive atmosphere which he had created for the tutoring sessions. At the conclusion of the school year, Billy scored only four months below the mean reading level established by his class on a traditionally administered achievement test. His behavior in school had become more outgoing and fights with classmates had lessened markedly. Billy's parents had noticed that he was much more relaxed at home since the tutoring program began.

Billy's program continued throughout the school year. Instructional objectives and sub-objectives were modified to reflect his learning needs, a sign of a good tutorial program. Billy's academic gains had effects in other areas. His relationship with peers and family improved noticeably. The specific reasons why this happened are unclear. Perhaps Billy felt better about himself because his classroom performance had improved. He may have felt better about himself because he felt that someone cared about how he was doing and was willing to continue to work with him over a period of time. Whatever the reason, Billy became a better student and changed his behavior with peers in a positive direction.

The preceding example illustrates several elements common to many tutorial programs. First, the need for the program arose from the student's academic limitations and the teacher's desire to remediate these limitations in an efficient manner. Second, the tutor was chosen because he was older, although not necessarily a better student. He did, however, possess the basic skills needed to administer each lesson. Although case-histories seldom mention this, the tutor often gains from the tutoring experience, whether by being more motivated academically or by being more sure of himself in the classroom.

The second example concerns Mr. Rowley, a first grade teacher who noticed that one of his students was experiencing great difficulty in mastering basic mathematical concepts. The child, Sam, would complete a lesson one day, and the next day not be able to do any of the problems that were introduced in the previous day's lesson. Even the aide, Mrs. Montgomery, could not get Sam to work on his lessons without some sign of "backsliding." Mr. Rowley talked with other teachers in his building and tried many of their suggestions. The strategies did not work. One day when Mrs.

Montgomery was not in class, Mr. Rowley asked an older student to stay in his class and work with some of the students. The student, Charles, gave an assignment to Sam. Mr. Rowley noticed that the two boys were working quietly on a lesson that Sam had earlier not been able to complete. Mr. Rowley decided to have Charles work with Sam on a daily basis following the lesson plan already established. Sam progressed speedily through all the pre-planned lessons and moved on to a new book, all in the space of a month. Apparently, Sam had been capable of performing at this level previously, but had not the motivation to work at a level commensurate with his ability.

The assistance that Charles gave to Sam can be called peer tutoring because in effect the pair covered material that was supplemental to as well as an integral part of the classroom program. The example also illustrates some of the added advantages of a tutoring program. The peer contact which the tutoring provides may add the spark needed to get certain students to try harder. The child being tutored may be more relaxed or comfortable working with a peer tutor, and thus better able to concentrate on learning materials. The tutor provides the student being tutored with increased individual attention, greater closeness and contact with the tutor, more immediate and frequent feedback on performance, and a peer model to emulate while progressing towards academic and/or social achievement. These advantages are very important to the learning process and will be discussed in much greater detail in a later chapter.

The next example concerns a research-oriented study conducted by one of the authors. A sixth-grade classroom in a parochial school was divided into two sections. Students good in spelling were trained over a two-day period to be tutors. Students who were not good spellers were chosen to be tutored in spelling. Although the details of the actual research were extensive and complicated, several points became clear over the course of the project. Children at the same grade level as well as in the same classroom *could* effectively work with each other in a tutorial setting. Children did not choose their partners, so many of the students were matched with students who were not their friends. In every instance, the pairs were able to complete their assigned work and complete lessons in the specified period.

The project lasted one month and consisted of twenty daily sessions. The experience of tutoring classmates was reported to be of value by the tutors. The students being tutored similarly expressed their positive feelings about the experience. The teachers in whose classrooms the program was conducted were not only pleased when their students' spelling abilities increased but also were surprised at how smoothly the pairs worked together. On several occasions, they approached the author with comments about a particular child's behavior while tutoring when this behavior was a pleasant surprise to the teachers. The students demonstrated that they could assist each other, even when their previous relationships with each other had contained friction.

The final example concerns the Youth Tutoring Youth (YTY) program in New York City. The YTY program was large-scale, both in the number of students who participated and in the amount of funds made available for its maintenance. The YTY had the following objective: improving, for the tutor and the child being tutored, the cognitive and affective results of learning activities (Deterline, 1970). Primary emphasis was on affective learning by the tutors. The YTY had most tutoring pairs working at cross-age and cross-grade levels. The typical tutor was an underachiever in a high school. Emphasis in tutoring sessions was placed on creating a warm and supportive environment in which the tutee could learn. William Glasser's Reality Therapy model was used to create such an environment for learning. The learning of instructional materials was secondary to the development of affective areas of the tutor and his or her partner. Games, field trips, and special projects provided the context for this learning.

The four examples discussed above, while differing in magnitude and scope, all support the idea that children can assist other children in the remediation of academic deficiencies. Other programs will be described in the text to further support the potential for the success of a peer tutorial program. Guidelines will be given to assist the teacher in establishing similar programs, or ones whose scope is vastly different. The programs can be shaped to meet the individual needs of both the student and teacher. The gains from such a program can be exciting and fruitful for all involved. In later chapters we will explore ways to maximize the chances of establishing a program that works in a particular classroom and school.

2
HISTORICAL PERSPECTIVES AND RESEARCH ON PEER TUTORING

The roots of peer tutoring can be traced to the developing needs of societies to educate their young in the necessary tasks that guarantee the continuation of the group. In ancient times, the concern of a group of individuals was with survival and the maintenance of physiological needs. In more recent history, with the development of formal systems devoted to the education of children and youth, emphasis has shifted to training students to meet the cognitive and affective demands of the larger society. Children teaching other children has occurred throughout the recorded history of mankind. This chapter will review some of the information available on early systems of peer tutoring, and then will proceed to discuss studies that have investigated the variables that affect the outcomes of peer tutoring programs.

HISTORICAL PERSPECTIVES

The first image that comes to mind when one thinks of children teaching other children is that of little red schoolhouses that were staffed by one dedicated teacher. As a result of having a variety of students to instruct, these teachers frequently relied on the older or more intelligent students to work with the other children. The genesis of peer tutoring, however, lies farther in the past. Bateson (1972) has described several "simple" societies that emphasized the early involvement of children in adult roles, including acting as teachers of younger children in the family. In societies in which a prolonged childhood as we know it does not exist, there is an expectation that the young, once weaned and walking, can assume familial responsibilities. Who better than other children to instruct them in the specifics of role responsibilities?

Gartner, Kohler and Riessman (1971), in an interesting review of early references to children teaching other children, have noted several discussions of the topic in preceding centuries. Particularly fascinating is the reference to John Comenius (whose work was first published in 1849) who recommended that the student who wanted to make progress in a subject should arrange to give lessons to others on a regular basis. Comenius mentions the phrase "He who teaches others, teaches himself" as supporting his belief. The learning advantages for the tutor in a tutorial arrangement receive additional mention from Andrew Bell (1832) who stated that he who teaches learns.

During the same period, Joseph Lancaster (1806) proposed the "monitoring system." Under his system, which was dictated by economic rather than educational factors, children were highly successful in teaching other children within his schools. This idea became popular for a time in the United States and set the stage for later, more ambitious, efforts in the area of peer tutoring.

William Bentley Fowle (1866) provided the educational theory to support peer tutorial practices. Like Lancaster, Fowle utilized the monitorial approach to education in his school. He believed that children who taught were better able to learn materials, because they were learning by reviewing, not merely memorizing. Fowle believed strongly that children were capable of communicating effectively to other students in a learning arrangement. He wrote that children can be better teachers than adults. Unlike adults, children are more likely to work democratically with their partners, constantly considering their partner's feelings and capacities. He labeled this teaching style as "learner-focused."

The ideas of Fowle, Lancaster and Bell were heard by American educators who, in common with their European counterparts, did not have much money with which to hire teachers in great numbers. When one teacher was hired to work with the children of an entire settlement or town, the teacher often would rely on certain students to teach others (Johnson, 1970). The arrangements seem to have been successful—many of our country's early leaders came from such schools. Modern day equivalents to these one-room experiments in learning have developed with many of the same justifications, economic and educational, that motivated these earlier class-room activities.

EARLY PEER TUTORIAL PROJECTS

Gartner, Kohler and Riessman (1971) are again an excellent source of information on the development of large-scale tutorial projects across the United States. Their interest in tutorial models is reflected by their participation in several of these projects. Much of the information on early projects is anecdotal in nature. Lippitt and Lohman (1965) authored one of the first studies that dealt with peer tutoring in the educational environment. This study, conducted in the early 1960s, was responsible for the creation of several tutorial projects designed to meet the academic needs of students. Beginning projects were cross-age in focus. Junior and senior high school students were tutoring elementary school students. Another project involved sixth graders working with kindergarten students. An additional project was started in a camp setting. The tutorial programs were based on several assumptions:

1   Younger children often model the behaviors (affective and attitudinal) of older children. This modeling can be utilized in an educational context when the models can be trained in appropriate behaviors.
2   The relationships that tutors establish with the adult support team affect these older children who have been trusted by adults on an important work assignment. Tutors also have the opportunity in the tutorial context to work on peer relationship skills.
3   Tutors, in their duties, are learning the materials more thoroughly than would normally occur in the traditional classroom.
4   Tutors are able to help tutor and tutee by participating in the academic portions of the program.

5   Tutors, through their work and their success with their part-
     ners, can become more sure of their academic and affective
     skills and interpersonal competencies.

Results of these early studies were quite positive. Lippitt and
Lohman (1965) reported that both tutor and tutee profited on
several dimensions following participation in a tutorial program.
Tutees increased scores on academic tests as well as on measures of
interest and motivation. Tutors also increased their ability to work
with other students and had more positive attitudes toward school.

An interesting extrapolation of the data from these earlier studies
is discussed by Gartner et al. (1971). They present five types of
children who seem to benefit from tutorial programs and other
student-to-student contacts. The children who benefited most were
those who had experienced previous failures in relating to peers,
"babies" in families, oldest children, children who had not had experience in working with others on an equal footing, and students
who had never worked with an older, same-sex child. A common
element noted among the five types of children is the lack of extensive and successful contact with peers.

One characteristic of these earlier efforts at peer tutoring was
that they utilized relatively few children and focused more extensively on affective rather than academic variables. Little attention
was devoted to developing specific instructional techniques but,
rather, the main goal was to demonstrate that the tutorial model can
work. Indeed, the peer tutoring programs, in general, appeared to be
quite successful. Soon larger projects involving tutoring were developed and implemented on a large scale.

Mobilization for Youth, an ambitious project, was begun in the
early 1960s in New York City. The project employed several centers
throughout the city where high school students tutored fourth and
fifth grade students in reading. Some students received two hours of
tutoring a week, and others four hours. Students in both the tutor
and tutee groups were typically black or Puerto Rican American.
Cloward (1967) reported that tutees who received the four hours
of tutoring a week made significant improvements in reading achievement. Children who had received two hours a week in tutoring also
made gains; however, they were not as great in magnitude as those
made by the four-hour-a-week students. Interestingly, tutors made

the most progress, gaining 3.4 years in reading ability in the seven months of sessions. Ability gains from tutoring did not immediately transfer to the classroom, at least as can be inferred from the students' subsequent grades. Project personnel predicted that future improvements would eventually be realized (Gartner, Kohler and Riessman, 1971).

Youth Tutoring Youth programs also were initiated in the Northeast, in such major cities as Newark and Philadelphia. An after-school program, YTY used high school-aged children enrolled in the Neighborhood Youth Corps and who were shown to be at least two years behind grade level in reading. These students were trained to tutor younger underachieving students in schools that served ghetto areas. Tutors were paid a salary for their time and worked out of community centers that were staffed by professional and paraprofessional educators who came from the same community. More important than the gains in reading scores that the tutors experienced were increases in the interest levels of these students for academic tasks. Tutors seemed to become "hooked" into the tutor role and would work on their own time to create new, interesting materials for their partners. The tutors' feelings of personal worth were apparently given a strong boost.

Newmark and Melaragno (1969) reported research findings of the System Development Corporation. In several schools both cross-age and same-age tutorial projects were conducted. In the former case, fifth and sixth graders tutored first graders, while in the latter instance, first graders tutored other first graders. The authors argued for the importance of what they labeled a tutorial community, in which all students would serve as both learners and teachers.

As in previous examples, the children who were involved in the tutorial program benefited. Tutors' academic motivation and interest increased, with an observable impact on their classroom behavior. The children who were being tutored exhibited academic gains and also appeared to be more in tune with the cognitive and affective demands of the classroom. Teachers were impressed with the impact of the tutorial program on their students. Teachers were pleased with the tutors' ability to assume responsibility of individualized work with students. The authors additionally stressed the need for future programs to attend to three factors in setting up a program:

training and support of tutors; allowing enough time for more adequate planning and development functions; greater parent involvement, so that community support would develop for their program.

An ambitious but small-scale tutorial program was described by Gartner et al. (1971), called Each One Teach One. The program, conducted in Yonkers, New York, was schoolwide in scope, at least in its initial stages. Students were tutored and served as tutors for most of the day. Goals of the program for the tutor and tutee were both affective and academic. They included increases in classroom skills, improvements in self-concept and self-esteem, improvements in peer relationships, and improvements in individualized attention to the needs of students. The program was successful in involving all students in the learning. The initially shy child became more active in peer relationships after a stint as a tutor. Children were able to learn through tutoring, and to become more encouraged with their abilities to perform academically.

The learning cell approach that was adopted in the late 1960s at McGill University is an example of a peer tutorial program at the college level. College students were working with each other to master the materials in a specific course. Students in the learning pairs often switched from teacher to learner roles with each other. This learning through teaching program was as successful as other learning options in preparing students for the content of the final examination. Students in the pairs enjoyed their arrangement more than did the students in the other course arrangements (more traditional approaches to instruction).

Another learning through teaching program was the Student Assistant program at a high school in Portland, Oregon. Students served as tutors, as well as helpers in a variety of school activities. One feature of the program was the tutoring of an entire class by an older group of students. The program was able to provide children with a series of successful learning experiences.

Gartner et al. (1971) have described three additional ventures into peer tutoring that proved equally successful. The programs were cross-age in their focus. In the first program, which was sponsored by Hunter College in New York City, college students tutored ten-year-olds who in turn tutored seven-year-olds. The college students were themselves training to be teachers. Four benefits were believed to result from this program:

1   Two sets of students were receiving tutorial assistance.
2   The self-esteem of the ten-year-olds, who served as tutors, was increased because of their ability to succeed in a learning environment.
3   The regular classroom teachers' work load was reduced with the addition of the college's program.
4   The college students were provided with the opportunity to observe a practical learning situation. With this background, the students would have a more reality-based grasp on the dynamics of learning arrangements.

The second program mentioned by Gartner and colleagues was an English program based upon the principles of the Youth Tutoring Youth program in the United States. Tutors, who ranged in age from 13 to 18, tutored other students who ranged in age from 6 to 12. The program lasted for six weeks and was concerned with the improvement of English language skills of the students, who were non-English-speaking Punjabis. Upon completion of the program, project staff discovered that both tutors and tutees made greater use of the English language, tutors felt better about themselves, and the community supported this type of program.

In a more peer-oriented program in New Jersey, students at the preschool level worked together in pairs to learn, prepare assignments, and to monitor each other's performance. Goals for the program were to increase language skills, including communication, and to reduce the teacher's load. The monitoring component of the program was important in that the students learned to help others learn and were able to review previous academic materials. So successful was the project that tutors in the program were interested in continuing the learning with partners approach when they moved from the preschool level.

The programs that we have discussed serve as an introduction to the variety of programs that have been implemented with the theme of children teaching other children. This introduction to the broad range of peer tutorial programs has contained several common factors in the studies. Programs in the great majority of instances were cross-age, rather than programs in which children of the same age or grade level tutored each other. Tutorial variables that have been investigated for their effects on outcomes from peer tutorial programs have been oriented towards product rather than process. We will examine some issues in the literature on peer tutoring after discussion of an interesting and effective variation of the tutoring approach.

PROGRAMMED TUTORING

Ellson and his colleagues at Indiana University have published two major studies on the programmed tutoring approach. Programmed tutoring involves close control of the behavior of the tutor and the learner, with very specific guidelines determining the manner in which lesson content is taught. Content is highly structured, with learning progression being in small steps. The material to be taught in the tutorial sessions is laid out for the tutor, as is the manner in which materials are to be presented (Ellson, Harris and Barber, 1968). In contrast, directed tutoring, using Ellson's terminology, consists of a set of activities and materials that are structured so that a person of average academic abilities could conduct a tutorial session with a student. In part, Ellson's research activities have been directed at assessing the relative merit of the two methods of tutoring.

Ellson, Barber, Engle and Kampwerth (1965) reported on ten experiments in which the technique of programmed tutoring was developed from a procedure to teach short lists of words to a technique of individualized teaching of elementary reading skills. Results of the experiments indicate that programmed tutoring, used as a supplement and coordinated with regular classroom teaching, is more effective than classroom teaching alone, and more effective than programmed tutoring alone. Programmed tutoring was found to be effective especially in teaching vocabulary and beginning reading skills to children who had had the greatest difficulty among their peers in acquiring such skills in class. The subjects in this 1965 study included black and white children from inner city schools.

Ellson et al. (1965) reported large differences in the mean rate at which children of different ages and educational histories learn to read using programmed tutoring. While early in tutorial sessions differences in learning rates existed among students in the studies, most children came to learn at about the same rate as fast learners by the end of the tutorial programs. The authors reported that among the students participating in the programmed tutoring projects, only severely retarded children failed to exhibit gains in learning.

In the Ellson studies, the optimal length of time to devote to a tutoring session was determined to be fifteen minutes. This span represents the influence of a child's attention span. The authors ran 240 children in twenty inner city schools through several variations of tutoring programs. Students were in the first grade and were tutored for an entire school year. Sessions were presented either once or twice a day in the morning. Some students were taught using directed tutoring, others using programmed tutoring. Directed tutoring adapts regular classroom techniques and materials to the individualized instruction of children in reading. Guidelines on the use of the materials were given to the tutors by experienced reading specialists. Underlying the directed tutoring activities was the assumption that the tutoring would provide the learner with reading activities that could occur in the regular classroom, *if* the teacher had the time to provide such activities. Programmed tutoring in the study consisted of several sub-programs: (1) sight-reading, or teaching words in a meaningful context, so that the child learns to read words as well as the sentences, phrases, or paragraphs in which the words occur; (2) free-reading, or the teaching of new words with less interruption to the reading process, so that the child can concentrate upon comprehension of the material; (3) word analysis or phonics, the use of context and grapheme–phoneme correspondence to pronounce and identify printed materials; and (4) comprehension, the understanding of reading content (Ellson et al., 1968).

Programmed tutoring emphasizes the successes of the learner by reinforcing correct responses with verbal praise, such as "Good," "That's right," and so on. The tutor does not respond verbally to mistakes by the learner. Rather the tutor directs repeated efforts at correcting the deficiencies. Absence of overt negative feedback is combined with working towards the learner's strengths, so that the learner becomes more confident with his or her abilities. This approach is considered by Ellson to be appropriate for slow learners, who receive a great deal of attention for their failures in learning rather than their successes. Ellson et al. (1968) reported that programmed tutoring twice a day for fifteen minutes per session resulted in significantly greater increases in reading achievements of children under these tutorial conditions than under directed tutoring conditions and less intensive programmed tutoring conditions. While reading scores for programmed tutored children were increased, the children with initially lower achievement were increased to a greater degree than was the case for their more successful classmates.

The Ellson studies differed from other tutorial studies in that the tutors were adult females who had graduated from high school. The tutors were well-trained in the specifics of the procedure for their work with their students. Also differing from other studies were the length of sessions and the tutorial content. Tutorial pairs met for either one or two sessions a day in the morning. The sessions lasted fifteen minutes, a time limit considered to be optimal for children in the first grade classrooms that were participating in the study. Content consisted of sight-reading materials, a statement comprehension program, and a problem word analysis program.

Ellson believes that for any type of tutoring to be effective it should be conducted in conjunction with a strong academic classroom program in the same subject area. Tutoring does not substitute for classroom learning; rather it can supplement teacher-directed learning activities. Developing a peer tutorial program that takes the place of regular instruction in a content area may lessen the chances of the eventual success of that program.

In addition, the authors observed that the programmed tutoring approach has many advantages over other types of tutoring. The principles can be taught quickly to volunteer adults. As a result of materials being highly structured, there is little variation in the manner in which they are presented to learners. Thus tutors can begin working with students after a brief training program. One obvious necessity of programmed tutoring is that program materials be highly sequenced and ordered to permit easy presentation.

Ellson et al. (1965) emphasized the "therapeutic" effect of programmed tutoring. Students in the programmed tutoring context can display abilities that have not been demonstrated in the classroom. Changes that occur in tutoring frequently extend into the regular classroom. At the least, children who have experienced success of learning by tutoring will feel more confident about their abilities to learn. Greater confidence can motivate them to try harder in the regular classroom.

Readers interested in learning more about the programmed tutoring approach are referred to Ellson et al. (1968) and Ellson et al. (1965). A number of school districts have employed the approach successfully. In many instances high school students have replaced adults as the tutors. The type of structure that is given to materials in programmed tutoring can be examined in Ellson et al. (1968).

RECENT STUDIES IN PEER TUTORING

Programs involving peer tutoring have been conducted with possibly every combination of cross-grade and age pairings, and with innumerable variations of other factors. For example, some studies have varied tutor factors, such as whether the tutor volunteered or was required to participate in a program. Other studies have paid some students and not others. Additional studies have investigated the effect of the tutor's achievement and intellectual level on the outcomes of tutoring sessions. Most of the studies that we will discuss in this section are cross-age tutorial in focus, rather than peer tutorial in a strict sense. On a cross-age level, college students have tutored other college students and students at lower educational levels (Etters, 1967; Snipes, 1971; Tillett, Porter and Joiner, 1972; Yuthas, 1970). High school students have tutored elementary school students (Bell, Garlock and Colella, 1969), and older elementary school children have tutored younger students (Hagen and Moeller, 1971).

Gartner and his colleagues (1971), mentioned in the previous section on early tutorial projects, placed peer tutoring within a broader continuum of activities in which students help other students in the classroom. These investigators reported observing one-to-one interactions between children in the classroom, children working as leaders of small groups, children acting as "big brother" or "big sister" to other students, and assuming a variety of roles responsive to the academic and affective needs of their peers. These activities can be described as peer tutoring in intent.

The student is an educational tool with great potential as an instructional agent. Thomas (1970) compared the behavior of college-aged tutors and that of fifth and sixth grade tutors working with second graders in a reading program. Not only were the student tutors as effective as the college education majors in producing reading gains for the second-grade children, but the student tutors were more direct and businesslike in their interactions with the tutees. They tended to focus upon the tasks at hand, while the education majors were more likely to play with and to coax along their charges. The student tutors were less likely than the college education majors to be distracted by the antics of their learning partners.

Teachers profit from the introduction of tutors in a variety of ways, as can be gleaned from references in the literature. The classroom teacher is freed to work as a manager of learning in the classroom, by assigning certain students the responsibility of directing instructional arrangements with other students. Gartner et al. (1971) suggest that the teacher can use the extra time to plan lessons, to consult with other staff on instructional matters, and to program materials for future tutorial sessions.

Reports on Benefits for the Tutee and Tutor

Benefits for the tutor and tutee can be extensive within the context of most peer tutoring activities. In fact, certain educators believe that benefits for the tutor can outweigh in importance benefits for the child being tutored. For the tutee, the child receives increased individual attention, greater closeness and contact with the instructional agent, more immediate and frequent feedback on performance, and a peer model to emulate. This modeling factor may be one of the most powerful change-inducing factors in the peer tutorial model. Children are able to observe another student who remains focused on the academic materials, who approaches the learning of materials in a calm and competent manner, and who is interested in helping the tutee learn. The child being tutored is very likely to exhibit a previously unobserved ability to grasp the instructional component of the tutoring and to acquire the learning behaviors of the partner. These skills are commonly transferred to the regular classroom to enable the tutee to experience greater academic success.

The fact that a tutee may be more relaxed with a peer tutor, and thus better able to concentrate on learning materials, is supported by a number of studies. Geiser (1969), Hassinger and Via (1969), Bouchillon and Bouchillon (1972), Fleming (1969), Landrum and Martin (1970), and Lippitt and Lohman (1965) have all reported increases in learning outcomes by tutees following a tutorial program. In these studies, student tutors have come from elementary, secondary and college grade levels. Snapp (1970) and Snapp,

Oakland and Williams (1972) reported improvements in tutee reading development following a cross-age tutorial program for elementary school children. Volunteers were utilized in the program, and the tutoring sessions were conducted before the start of the school day.

Gains experienced by the children being tutored have been reported to transfer to the regular classroom (Gartner et al., 1971). Cloward (1967), however, reported on a cross-age tutoring component of the Mobilization for Youth program in which gains in reading following a tutorial program did not result in better reading achievement in the classroom.

Gains in self-concept also have been reported for tutees who have recently completed a tutorial program. Ross (1972), in a program that required students labeled "disadvantaged" to tutor similarly classified students, reported that gains in reading scores and self-concept followed a semester-long program of peer tutoring. The tutors were second-semester students in a compensatory basic studies program, while tutees were in their first semester in the program. Greatest gains were experienced by tutors who had themselves been tutees in previous semesters and by their tutees. Overall, students made better reading and self-concept gains when acting as tutors than when acting as tutees.

Other studies have reported on learning gains for tutors, while a few studies have failed to discover significant and measureable changes. McWhorter and Levy (1970), reporting on college-level, low-reading-ability tutors of elementary-level, low-reading-ability tutees, noted gains of 2.4 years in reading ability for tutors following one semester of tutoring in reading. High school tutors have been reported to gain also in scores on reading achievement tests after working with elementary school-aged children on reading (Cloward, 1967). Lederman (1974) proposed that tutoring experiences sharpen the abilities of the tutor in the subject area taught. Geiser (1969) and Fleming (1969) make the same claims of tutor benefits for children at the elementary school level.

Snapp et al. (1972) did not find significant differences between tutors and their controls on Metropolitan Achievement Test scores and Teacher Ratings following a tutorial program in reading. Horan, deGirolomo, Hill and Shute (1974) argued that many other studies have failed to produce much support on tutorial benefits for the tutor, especially benefits for these students in learning. Horan and colleagues present evidence favoring tutor gains in class attitude and behavior. Such changes in the tutor's behavior are likely to carry over to other areas of the child's performance. The student who feels more competent and better able to cope with the demands of teaching another student probably will maintain this heightened confidence in nontutorial academic settings.

Dahlen (1973) conducted a study in which high school students tutored third graders. Following a program of tutoring towards reading objectives, he found that tutors of the same sex as the tutee have greater influence on outcome scores in reading than do tutors of the opposite sex of the tutee. Children with same-sex tutors scored higher on reading posttests than did the children in the cross-sex pairs. No similar effects were found for tutoring in arithmetic. Apparently, sex of tutorial partner can affect learning outcomes under certain conditions.

Same-Age Tutorial Programs

Programs that have utilized tutors who are the classmates of tutees seldom are cited in the literature. Oakland and Williams (1975), working at an elementary school, reported gains in word knowledge and reading comprehension by tutees taught solely by tutors. The reading achievement outcomes of children receiving peer tutoring were not particularly different from those of children receiving instruction from the classroom teacher. The use of peer tutors to supplement teacher instruction produced better outcomes in learning for the tutees, although improvements were not statistically significant. Ellson, Barber, Engle and Kampwerth (1965) also have mentioned the advantages of tutoring being designed to supplement classroom instruction.

Some additional studies that have reported on same-grade level peer tutorial programs include those of Ross (1972), with a college group of students in a remedial basic studies program, and of Vassallo (1973), with a high school peer tutoring program. Hamblin and Hamblin (1972) described a unique peer tutoring program developed for preschool-age children. Peer tutors were chosen from children in the group who could learn more rapidly than others of their peers on some experimental reading materials. The authors reported substantial and significant improvement in the rate at which students learned to read following peer tutoring and rewards for reading.

Ehly and Larsen (1976) discussed the results of a peer tutorial program, in which sixth graders tutored their classmates on experimental materials in spelling. Student pairs met for twenty sessions, each of which lasted thirty minutes. The effects of a variety of tutor and tutee characteristics on the learning of tutees were analyzed. The authors found that sex of tutor, sex of tutee, type of sex pairing (same-sex versus opposite-sex pairing), peer acceptance and peer rejection of the tutor and tutee, tutor liking for the tutee, and tutee liking for the tutor did not affect at a significant level the outcome learning scores of the students being tutored. Examination of the data revealed that the only significant predictor of the amount of learning by the tutee was that student's pretutorial spelling score on a test which assessed the tutee's knowledge of the content of the program. None of the tutor and tutee characteristic factors listed above was found to predict the learning efficiency of tutorial pairs, that is, the speed with which the partners completed their daily assignments.

Peer tutoring programs have differed widely in the structuring of the materials presented to the child being tutored. Many studies have encouraged the tutor to improvise activities on a particular subject. Inversely, some programs are highly structured as represented by programmed tutoring (White, 1971). In programmed tutoring, both the sequencing and content of instructional materials are prespecified by the classroom teacher or the project director. Ellson, Harris, and Barber (1968) have argued that all aspects of the operational program, including practice and review, are highly responsive to the learner's interactions with the materials under this tutorial arrangement. Programmed tutoring emphasizes the successes of the tutee by reinforcing correct responses with verbal praise. Failures are not responded to verbally, but rather result in repeated efforts directed at correcting errors.

Tutorial programs have differed in the reinforcement systems built into the program content, and have varied in the amount of feedback that is provided to the child being tutored on his or her success. An example of an approach that provides very specific feedback to the tutee is that of Peer Mediated Instruction (PMI). Building on the instructional programming processes of Computer-Assisted-Instruction procedures, Rosenbaum (1973) proposed the PMI concept, that allows students to work in pairs, with one student designated as the teacher and one as the learner. The "teacher" presents materials, such as words from a spelling list, to the student, then provides specific correction to student errors. The correction process involves the "teacher" comparing the student's responses with an answer key before presenting the correction. Rosenbaum has structured the immediate selective correctional procedures to be similar to the "partial answer feedback" process of IBM computer-generated programs. Correction specifies exactly where the error occurs, then allows repeated attempts by the student to correct the answer. Total feedback on the correct response is structured so that the learner can incorporate these data at a later trial. Results from a PMI program in spelling have been positive. Third graders were able to increase spelling scores when they were instructed with the PMI technique. The PMI technique has been reported to be successful in tutorial programs that focused on other content areas.

Ehly (1975) conducted a peer tutorial program in spelling that utilized the PMI approach of providing feedback to the child being tutored. In this study, sixth graders tutored each other on spelling words that had been missed on a pretest by all of the tutees. The PMI approach was effective in providing the tutor with the structure necessary to conduct tutorial sessions and in maintaining the tutees' interest throughout the course of the project, which lasted for twenty sessions. Tutees did learn to spell many of the difficult words during the PMI-oriented sessions. Greater detail on this study is provided in Chapters 4 and 5.

To summarize, studies in peer tutoring same-grade or same-age tutoring programs are reported infrequently in the literature. More often mentioned are studies on cross-age tutoring. Benefits for tutors and tutees frequently follow participation in a tutorial program. These benefits can transfer to the regular classroom. Tutorial partners can work productively together regardless of their ages, sex, racial-ethnic status, and intelligence levels. Structuring of content and presentation of materials have varied widely across studies. The more structured approaches, such as the PMI approach and programmed tutoring, can produce learning gains for the child being tutored.

Process Factors in Peer Tutoring

Very few studies have attempted to answer the question of why tutoring works. Variables reflecting some process factors that may be operating with peer tutorial interactions have been discussed by Little and Walker (1968). In a college program that employed group tutorials, the investigators reported on characteristics of the tutorial relationships that were related to achievement outcomes in psychology (the tutorial content) for tutees. Little and Walker had modified Lewis, Lovell and Jessee's (1965) Teacher Pupil Relationship Inventory (TPRI) to reflect the dynamics of tutor-tutee relationships. Factor-analyzing student responses to the modified TPRI, Little and Walker discovered four factors to account for a large portion of the variance in the tutees' responses. These factors were likeableness, status, personal involvement, and relationship control. High scorers on the "status" factor saw the tutorial relationship as one between equals. High scorers on the "personal involvement" factor saw the tutor as willing to become involved personally with the tutee. High scorers on the "relationship control" factor thought that control of what was happening in the relationship was shared between tutor and tutee. Little and Walker, upon analyzing all data, reported that only the "likeableness" factor was correlated significantly with outcome achievement of the tutees. The authors were forced to conclude that they could not provide strong support for the contention that interpersonal relationship qualities are important in teaching arrangements similar to group tutorials.

Ehly (1975) investigated some tutorial process factors in his study. He consulted the literature on teacher-student classroom interaction factors and the peer tutorial studies mentioned above before developing an hypothesis on the relationship of tutor-tutee process effects to learning outcomes from peer tutoring. His hypothesis is illustrated in Figure 2-1.

Ehly investigated the interrelationships of several tutor and tutee characteristics, tutorial process factors, and tutee outcome factors. The characteristics studied were sex of partners, type of sex pairing (same-sex versus opposite-sex tutorial pairs), peer status of the partners, spelling pretest scores of the partners (ability estimate), liking of the partners for each other, age of the students, and some combination measures of the attributes related to peer status. Process

FIGURE 2-1. Conceptualization of Hypothesized Effects of
Major Variables

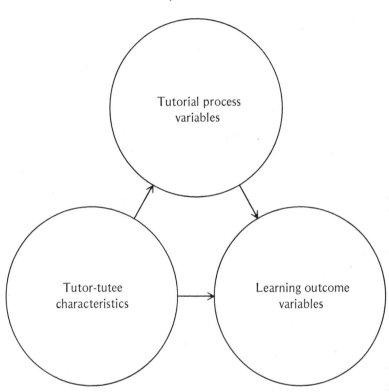

factors investigated were perceived competency and effect of the
tutor (as perceived by the tutee), perceived competency and effect
of the tutee (as perceived by the tutor), changes in the liking of the
partners for each other, and several combination measures of the
process factors listed. Learning outcome measures for the tutee were
scores on a spelling posttest, scores on a test of generalization of
learning, and learning efficiency scores of the pairs.

The findings indicated that tutee pretutorial spelling score was the
sole tutor-tutee characteristic predictive of the learning outcomes
tutee post-tutorial spelling score and score on the test of generalization. The tutoring helped children learn to spell, but did not alter
the spelling abilities of the child in relation to the rest of the class.
There was only one tutorial process predictor of a learning outcome.
The process factor represented a combination of several tutorial

process scores. Tutorial pairs in which the tutor and tutee rated each other similarly on perceived competency and perceived effect tended to spend more time in learning to spell each word. Pairs in which there was a large gap in the competency and effect totals were more likely to learn words in a shorter amount of time.

Tutor-tutee characteristics were more frequent predictors of tutorial process variables. Sex of tutor and sex of tutee, however, were not predictive of any process variable. The tutor's liking of the tutee was a predictor of the perceived competency score assigned by the tutee. A tutor who liked his tutee was perceived by the partner as a good tutor. The tutor who did not like his tutee was perceived as not being a good tutor. Apparently, the tutor characteristic of liking for the tutee was related to the subsequent process of the tutorial sessions. Type of sex pairing was predictive of changes in the liking score of the tutee for the tutor, with same-sex pairs being more conducive than opposite-sex pairs to the tutee "liking" his partner following the series of interactions.

The reader who examines the existing literature on process and product factors in peer tutoring will be continually impressed by the relatively few studies that have focused on the dynamics of an actual tutorial arrangement. Future studies should be devoted to the investigation of the actual processes of successful peer tutorial situations. Tutorial programs with same-grade peers need to be intensively investigated, as research on such programs remains very limited. If a better understanding of the processes of the tutorial relationship can be determined, it will assist in shaping programs and training tutors in more effective and productive directions. With such efforts, it is far more likely that the meaningful affective and cognitive gains of students will be realized.

SUMMARY

Same-grade peer tutoring programs seldom are mentioned in the literature on peer tutoring. More frequently mentioned are studies of cross-age tutoring. Peer tutoring programs are able to produce learning gains for both the tutor and the learner. There is some disagreement among investigators on the extent to which these gains will transfer to the regular classroom. In previous studies, male and female students have been assigned to tutorial pairs without regard to their sex. In one exception to this procedure, Dahlen (1973) reported better outcomes for learners in a same-sex, versus an opposite-sex, dyadic relationship. Structuring of content and the manner in which content is presented to learners have varied across studies. More structured programs, including the Peer Mediated Instruction approach, have produced significant gains in learning by tutored students.

Very little research has been directed at the examination of process factors during tutoring activities. Ehly (1975) reported in his study on process factors in tutoring that only a combination of his process factors was a significant predictor of learning outcome in his peer tutoring program. The investigation of process factors during peer tutoring remains a generally unexplored area of educational research.

3
INITIAL CONSIDERATIONS
IN ESTABLISHING
A PEER TUTORING PROGRAM

The teacher attempting to initiate a peer tutoring program either in an individual classroom or an entire school is immediately confronted with a series of obviously difficult decisions. In general, there are several key considerations that need to be taken into account when attempting to structure a given program. These considerations include: (1) the goals of the peer tutoring program; (2) selection of the most appropriate tutees; (3) selection and training of the tutors; and (4) the criteria to be employed when pairing the tutors and tutees. The purpose of this chapter is to discuss each of these issues as they pertain to the successful management of all peer tutoring activities.

GOALS OF THE PEER TUTORING PROGRAM

The goals that are established for a peer tutoring program will be little different regardless of whether only a few students are selected to participate or a schoolwide program is being considered. In general, the teacher will need to determine the broad categories of academic and social-emotional development most appropriate to the tutor and/or the child being tutored. The following two sections of this chapter will delineate the general goals for both categories of students.

Goals for the Tutor

Creating goals for tutors in a tutorial program probably will occur at two points: (1) before tutors are selected, and when project staff have determined the philosophy of the program; and (2) after tutors are selected, when staff can focus on the specific needs of each tutor. Program goals usually provide a broad focus that relates to both instruction and behavior.

Instructional Goals. When the intent of the tutorial program focuses on changing the tutor's instructional performance, goals can be defined that are specific to this aspect of the tutor's functioning. For example, one goal that is definitely associated with academic subject matter would be that students being tutored will gain one grade level in reading scores on a standardized test following completion of the tutorial program. A goal for tutors could be that they present materials to their partners in a predetermined sequence on each occasion that they meet. The tutor who fulfills this goal will be likely to return to the regular classroom with better learning habits and/or a more positive attitude towards participating in classroom activities. Addendum A illustrates sample tutorial objectives and how objectives were specified for use in the tutorial sessions.

Students of varying intellectual levels can tutor successfully. Most teachers can readily identify pupils who possess average or above-average intellectual capacity but who are achieving below grade level. These students seem not to have acquired the "spark" to learn either independently or following the leads of the teacher. It is apparent that for such students progress in mastering basic academic tasks will deteriorate unless learning can be made to be a more attractive enterprise. Concerned teachers work hard to motivate such students. With the availability of peer tutoring, teachers may have a tool to involve the student more intimately in the learning process. Several authors have commented on the learning gains experienced by tutors who have worked in tutorial programs at both the college and high school level (McWhorter and Levy, 1970; Cloward, 1967). One study found that low-reading-ability, college-level tutors of elementary-level, low-reading-ability tutees gained 2.4 years on a standardized test of reading ability following one semester of tutoring in reading (McWhorter and Levy, 1970). High school-aged tutors have been reported to gain in reading achievement after working with elementary-aged tutees on reading (Cloward, 1967). It is apparent that tutoring has great potential in enhancing the academic abilities of the tutor in the subject taught. Many teachers have reported gains among elementary-school-aged *tutors.*

Peer tutoring may serve to boost the academic performance of the student tutor who has had academic problems. Whether the increases in performance come from a "sharpening of skills" or from an increased interest in learning, the tutor can benefit in his role as instructional leader. Teachers should keep this fact in mind when selecting students to tutor.

The unmotivated learner can benefit academically by serving in the role of a tutor. Teachers have found that their best students can develop a better grasp of learning concepts after presenting academic content to a tutee. Above-average students are chosen by many teachers to fill tutor slots in programs, because these students are usually easier to train to tutor students on the same grade level as well as at lower grade levels. The teacher who is designing a "peer" tutoring program may choose, because of the needs and goals of the program, to select only such students for tutor programs.

Behavioral Goals.   Behavioral goals for the tutor reflect the social-emotional climate of the classroom and the behavioral patterns of the children in the tutorial program. When a program goal is for tutors to establish a warm and supportive atmosphere while tutoring, the objective (typically a more specific and concise statement of a desired outcome) for tutors may state that they exhibit reflective listening on at least 80 percent of observed occasions. Another objective could be that tutors maintain eye contact with their partners while talking. The creation of such goals for tutors will reflect the current academic and effective abilities of these students and the teacher's expectations for continued performance in these areas.

The prospect of social-emotional benefits for tutors was apparent in the example of selecting the unmotivated student to serve as a tutor. Another social-emotional benefit can be to involve a shy, withdrawn student in peer tutoring. Such a student, when placed in the relatively structured context of a peer tutorial relationship, will become more attentive to the needs of others and more willing to become involved in attempting to meet these needs. Teachers have frequently reported that shy students become more outgoing and willing to talk to other students after tutoring a classmate.

An example of this benefit of peer tutoring is provided from the experiences of one of the authors. Juanita, a very quiet sixth grader, was described by her teachers as a good student who seldom talked to teachers or other students. When Juanita was asked direct questions by the teachers, she would answer in a whisper. She did not volunteer for any group activities and, when placed in a group, would not talk with the other group members. When selected to participate in a large research project in peer tutoring, Juanita was chosen to be a tutor. After expressing some hesitation, she was matched with a male classmate to form a tutorial pair. Due to the structure of the tutorial program, Juanita followed a set format in presenting materials and in rewarding her partner for correct responses. Teachers observed Juanita during the tutorial sessions and noted that she was speaking much louder than her previous whispers. By the end of the tutoring sessions, which lasted for one month, Juanita was speaking in a conversational tone both in the tutoring sessions and in the classroom. She began to volunteer answers in front of the class. Her participation in groups became more verbal and outgoing. The teachers noted that Juanita's new openness was being reinforced by an increase in peer attention (Ehly, 1975).

Whether the behavioral changes evidenced by Juanita were related to her participation as a tutor in the project or whether other factors contributed to her greater openness is impossible to determine with certainty. However, it was thought that the dynamics in the peer tutoring positively affected her behavior. Specifically, the tutoring arrangement invariably provides continual feedback to the tutor that he or she is having a significant effect on another person. In essence, the tutor is helping another person to *learn*. In Juanita's case, being able to help another proved to be a very powerful activity. Similar experiences can commonly have a heavy impact on changing the subsequent behavior of the tutor. An important element in the tutoring process mentioned above is that Juanita was continually being rewarded for being verbal and directive. Her partner responded to her lead, placing Juanita in control of the learning process. The feeling of being in control of a learning situation can be very rewarding for any child. As a natural consequence of being in control, Juanita likely became more self-confident and began to exhibit more verbal behavior and to take a more directive role with others in the classroom.

The teachers reading this section should consider, in some detail, the diverse social-emotional needs of their students. If the behavior that a teacher desires to see in the child can be defined, then goals for that student can be incorporated into the design of a peer tutorial program. Only the teacher's imagination and creativity can limit the potential of the tutorial experience to meet the social-emotional needs of the tutor.

Goals for the Tutee

The development of goals for children who will be tutored also can occur at two points; both before and after tutees have been selected. *Pre-selection* goals will coincide with the broader program goals, and will be instructional or behavioral in scope. *Post-selection* goals are more specific to the individual needs of each tutee. Goals for the child can be instructional or behavioral.

Instructional Goals. Instructional goals for tutees often take the form of "Tutees will attain mastery of the tutorial materials by the end of the ten weeks of daily sessions." Degree of mastery exhibited in individual sessions will be specified as an objective. Expectations for individual tutees may vary to meet differences in ability level and differences in tutorial content. The children being tutored are seldom working at the same point on the same materials. Tutee goals should reflect these differences.

Meeting the academic needs of a student is the typical reason given for selecting a student to be tutored. Increased academic performance is usually one benefit derived from the experience for the tutee, who is receiving increased individual attention, greater closeness and contact with the instructor, more immediate and frequent feedback on performance, and a peer model to emulate. All of these factors are thought to contribute to learning gains by the child being tutored. The child may be more relaxed with a peer tutor and thus better able to concentrate on learning tasks. Several studies have reported increases in the learning outcomes for tutees following completion of a tutorial program (Geiser, 1969; Hassinger and Via, 1969; Bouchillon and Bouchillon, 1972;

and Fleming, 1969). In these studies, the tutors have been a variety of ages and from widely different grades and ability levels. Other studies have tested hypotheses on the effects of tutorial *process* factors on the learning of the tutor and tutee. Careful review of these studies in Chapter 2 should aid the teacher in establishing insight into constructing programs in individual classrooms or schools.

Behavioral Goals. The second broad area of tutorial benefits for the tutee includes meeting the social-emotional needs of the child to be tutored. As in situations described for tutors, the teacher may make a decision on who should be tutored on the basis of the social-emotional needs of the children in a classroom. As many teachers can testify, the social and emotional needs of the student are closely tied to the academic performance of that student. The teacher may decide to place the student who has been observed to withdraw from an adult teacher with a peer tutor for certain periods during the day. The child may immediately begin to talk and perform work for the peer tutor when in the past that student would have avoided working. The structure of multi-grade-level schools provides for the availability of older students who can come into classrooms to serve as teacher aides and tutors for other children. If in the process of tutoring the tutee becomes more willing to work, more willing to express himself, the potential of tutorial arrangements will have been realized. Again, the sensitive teacher is limited only by his or her creativity and imagination in structuring the tutorial experience to meet the needs of the child.

A behavioral objective for the students being tutored may be both group and/or individual in nature. An example of a group-level objective is that tutees stay on task for the duration of each tutoring session. "On task" can be defined as looking at materials, holding pencils in a writing position, and answering each question when it is asked. An objective for an individual student may be to complete a specific number of problems per session. An additional objective could be for the tutee to sit without squirming during sessions. Objectives for the children to be tutored will target instructional and affective potentials that the teacher believes can be realized within the context of the peer tutoring program.

PROCEDURES FOR ATTAINING GOALS
ESTABLISHED FOR THE TUTOR AND TUTEE

Once the teacher has selected the students who will participate in the tutorial program, the teacher is faced with choosing the most appropriate tasks for the learner, whether that child is the tutor or the child being tutored. The child's abilities and needs are, of course, the key to the decision. His or her immediate and developing needs can be met as the primary goals of the peer tutoring arrangement. For example, Billy, who is experiencing great difficulty in arithmetic, appears greatly in need of additional work on basic addition and subtraction facts. Peer tutoring seems to be an effective vehicle to provide this mode of input. The teacher has noticed that Billy's feelings about himself as a student and as a person may have been influenced by his performance in arithmetic, and, consequently, are of concern. The peer tutoring program may subsequently be structured to provide Billy with a large amount of feedback not only reflecting his performance but also his worth as a human being. The teacher may be the best equipped of school personnel to specify just what should be incorporated and emphasized in a peer tutorial program.

For several reasons, goals for the tutee and for the tutor are best determined before the peer tutoring begins. First, the materials and structure of the tutoring must be guided by the stated goals. Secondly, pretutorial assessment of needs and the creation of goals helps the teacher to determine when progress has been made by the partners during tutoring. The establishment of goals and objectives and the development of procedures to assess their attainment are critical components in evaluation efforts in the tutoring program. The more specific the objectives developed from the goals, the more specific the evaluation measures can be.

Setting up goals for the tutor and the child being tutored can be a learning experience for the teacher, child, and others involved in the process. The teacher may be aware of the learning and social-emotional needs of the child, but not aware that the child can frequently verbalize his or her needs quite accurately. The child, in a one-to-one discussion with the teacher, may provide data on needs that can be met through a tutorial program. Parents who are interested in the school performance of their children are excellent sources of information on the needs of their children. Many schools have developed a policy of involving parents in needs assessments for their children. The schools have worked closely with parents to inform them of the proposed entry of their child into a peer tutoring program. Parents appreciate and sometimes demand reports on the progress of their children in a tutorial program. If one of the components of your peer tutoring program is research, teachers need to acquaint themselves with their school system's policy for the procedures to be employed in research studies. Some school districts require the written consent of every parent who has a child participating in a research study.

Other school personnel may be valuable sources of information on the children's behavior as it may be reflected in the development of goals and objectives for a tutorial program. In middle and high schools, where students typically interact with different instructors during consecutive class periods, it is possible to check with them on the feasibility of various tutorial goals for a particular student. Many teachers who have developed a peer tutoring program for their school meet as a group to establish goals and objectives for students prior to their entry into tutoring.

One arrangement frequently employed in peer tutoring is to write a "contract" with the students pertaining to the objectives for each session. Using this approach, the teacher and child work together to define what will be expected of the student, how he or she will know when they have attained each objective, and what will result from meeting objectives. This type of arrangement is frequently very rewarding to the tutee and facilitates the establishment of an ongoing systematic schedule of positive reinforcement.

The evaluation of goal attainment, as earlier mentioned, is important both for determining the student's performance and for determining the utility and value of the overall peer tutoring program. The key to the entire evaluation effort is specifying as succinctly and clearly as possible the objectives for the student tutor and/or learner. Approaches such as that of Rosenbaum's Peer Mediated Instruction recommend that the presentation of materials proceed directly from the specific objectives that have been generated for the particular program (Rosenbaum, 1973). Other peer tutoring activities are less structured and require innovation by the teacher regarding the program content. Chapter 5 is devoted to determining the content of a peer tutoring program.

The teacher will experience greater success in being able to verify the attainment of program objectives if these objectives are defined in specific terms. The example of Billy, mentioned in Chapter 1, illustrates the benefit of stating objectives in behavioral terms. While this example refers to one instance of a child's need for remedial instruction, other situations require varying degrees of specification regarding behavioral objectives. For example, a tutoring program in mathematics may have as its daily objective the successful completion of each problem presented to the pupil being tutored. Several tutorial programs observed by the authors contained similar objectives. Students were assisted by the tutors until every problem had been successfully completed on at least one attempt. No limit was placed on the number of attempts allowed. Other programs have as their objective an arbitrary quota of work to be completed in each session and the acceptable number of correct responses to be made by the tutee. To illustrate, a program may specify that the student work with the tutor on three pages of materials and complete at least 80% of the material correctly. The teacher or teachers who are responsible for the creation of the tutorial program can determine the most appropriate or convenient standards for quantity and quality of output at any point prior to the start of the tutoring sessions. Programs which have had well-defined instructional and behavioral objectives for tutees as well as tutors have the greatest likelihood of being successful.

When attempting to meet the social-emotional needs of the students in the tutorial program, the teacher may experience difficulty in defining objectives in behavioral terms. One way to specify objectives involves standardized measures of self-concept, self-esteem, and other affective variables. The objective may be for the child to score in a more positive direction on some affective scale after participating in a tutoring program. Such measures are of value especially in evaluations of relatively large tutorial programs. However, the objectives of the classroom teacher seeking changes in the behavior of a child may be specified in another manner. The teacher can develop a list of how he or she would like the student to behave. For example, Beverly, a third grader, seldom looks at peers when talking, infrequently initiates conversations, and has not been known to smile in the school environment. With a list of objectives to increase the frequency of these behaviors, and with a tutor who is carefully trained in the attainment of program objectives, Beverly can be encouraged to look at the tutor when talking, initiate conversations, and smile at the tutor. Principles of operant conditioning are particularly well suited in those situations where specific behaviors can be maintained and rewarded. Interested readers are urged to consult Hall (1971), Cartwright and Cartwright (1974), and Gordon (1966) for helpful guides on the efficient observation and reinforcement of desired behaviors.

The particular task of the teacher in a peer tutoring program is to create goals for the students, specify objectives that reflect these goals, determine methods that will best attain the objectives, and establish procedures to assess the attainment of the objectives.

Deterline (1970) developed a "systems approach" to tutoring that incorporates many of the task components involved in setting up a program. The model is shown in Figure 3.1. This systems approach combined elements of specifying objectives that meet tutorial goals (as contained in test items), methods to attain objectives (tutoring sessions), and procedures to assess attainment of objectives (session posttests).

Cohen et al. (1972) developed a "roadmap for tutoring" that also combines many of the elements that we have presented as contributing to the success of the tutoring program.

Objectives usually can be established readily for the child who is soon to be tutored. The needs of a child can be verbalized clearly by many teachers, and thus be brought to bear on the creation of goals and objectives. The needs of the child who will be doing the tutoring often are not considered by the teacher. The teacher may be focusing only on the needs of the child to be tutored, and not even attempting to evaluate the program's effect on the tutor. In this case, the teacher needs to consider the match of the students in the tutorial arrangement on the basis of how well the children can work together. The teacher may attempt to assess the effects of the program on the tutor as well as the child being tutored.

The goals established for the tutor and for the child to be tutored must form a coherent and realistic package—coherent in that the attainment of goals by either partner must not interfere with the attainment of goals by the other partner, and realistic in that expectations for changes in the tutor are lower than those expected for the child to be tutored. By definition, the tutor is giving and the child

FIGURE 3.1. Systems Approach to Tutoring

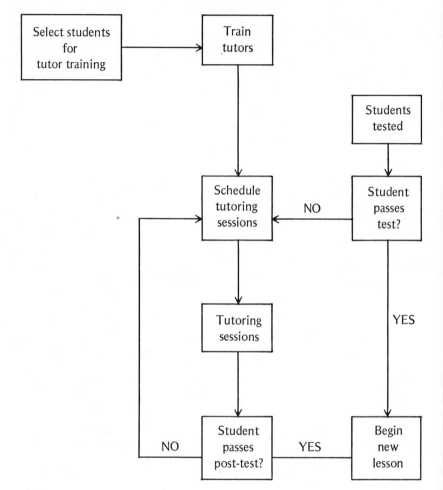

Source: Deterline, W.C., *Training and management of student-tutors. Final Report.* Palo Alto, Calif.: General Programmed Teaching, 1970. Used with permission of publisher.

being tutored is receiving. Modifications in the behavior of the tutor almost always are experienced later in the tutorial program than is the case for the children being tutored. David Klaus (1975) has reported that academic gains for the tutor are more likely to occur when the tutorial program's structure obliges the tutor to work with and to manipulate the instructional content, an experience that the teacher can program into the demands on the tutor. Klaus also found

"ROADMAP FOR TUTORING"

The Tutor	*The Tutee*
The tutor brings a repertoire of ideas and activities designed to help the tutee in specific areas.	The tutee brings a background of interests and abilities and a particular set of learning problems.
The tutor develops a *personal* relationship with the tutee, based on concern and respect for the tutee.	The tutee experiences a nonthreatening situation and a sense of self-respect and confidence.
The tutor uses various techniques, such as questioning and reinforcement, to diagnose problems and to encourage new learning.	The tutee uses his past successes in learning as a basis for mastering material in new and more difficult areas.
The tutor employs a variety of materials, designed both to develop interest and to enrich the learning experience.	The tutee learns new material in the context of his own interests and abilities.

MEANINGFUL LEARNING

Source: A.D. Cohen, J.C. Kirk, and W.P. Dickson. *Guidebook for tutors with an emphasis on tutoring minority children.* Stanford: Stanford University, Col. Comm. on Linguistics, 1972. Used with permission of publisher.

that academic gains for the child being tutored are more often produced in programs that very explicitly define the content, sequence, and procedure for each lesson. One additional finding by Klaus emphasizes the need to separate and control for the effects of academic objectives from those of social-emotional objectives in a program. He found that social growth seems more probable when emphasis on lesson content is removed and the partners are shown how to focus on each other's strengths instead of their weaknesses. The student tutor, faced with the responsibility of providing instruction as well as a warm supportive atmosphere during tutoring, may not be sure enough in the tutor role to accomplish both demands. As many teachers have observed, students tend to mimic the behaviors of their teachers while tutoring. Oftentimes, the behaviors they are copying are not the desired ones for the tutorial programs' objectives. Undoubtedly, the careful selection and training of students as tutors is a crucial element in a tutorial program.

SELECTING STUDENTS TO BE TUTORED

Just as specifying goals and objectives for the tutorial program is important for its success, it also is important that those students who are the best candidates for tutoring be selected for participation. In many tutoring programs, the overall goals established for the program determine the criteria by which students are selected. For example, in one program, teachers in an elementary school became concerned about the potential performance of their students on a statewide reading test. Knowing which students required remedial attention in reading and the amount of time before the date of administration for the test, the teachers selected those students who would be most likely to attain proficiency in the reading skill areas covered by the test. While such pressures are not uncommon in the creation of a peer tutoring program, the program's goals can influence selection procedures in a variety of ways. If a program employs cross-age tutoring, the teacher needs to consider the consequences of matching younger students with older ones. Such consequences are usually minimal. When the teacher is selecting students from the same grade level to be either tutors or learners, the selection decision becomes more complicated. The teacher sensitive to the current relationships of the learner to other students has to decide whether an actual peer will be the best possible tutor for the learner. A student who is very aware of his or her academic deficiencies may openly reject being placed with a classmate for tutoring.

There are two basic factors to consider before selecting any student to receive tutoring. The first factor is concerned with the *potential* of that student to exhibit change in his or her academic performance. While the peer tutoring program may be structured to accommodate demands on the student to the student's level of ability, there is no guarantee that the student will be either receptive to the tutoring or will experience academic gains simply as a result of tutoring. Some teachers would not consider selecting the student with severe learning handicaps. However, many teachers have reported the encouraging fact that children in special education programs and state schools for the mentally retarded have successfully learned within the context of peer tutoring. Many of these students were being tutored by other members of the same special education classes and state school programs. It appears that learning capability cannot by itself lessen the chances of a child to learn while participating in a tutorial program. The learning may proceed at a slower pace for some students, but academic goals can be achieved.

The second basic factor thus becomes critical. This factor is concerned with the *student's attitudes* and *beliefs* about *himself* or *herself*. These beliefs are typically exhibited in the student's social-emotional behavior. The student who is severely lacking in self-confidence may be targeted for peer tutoring. The program may focus on boosting that child's self-confidence through a process of providing the pupil with large quantities of success. However, the peer tutoring program is not usually considered a therapeutic tool. The potential for change by the tutee in social-emotional behavior is limited by several factors. The primary factor is the skill of the tutor to communicate effectively with and to motivate the mildly to moderately disturbed child.

One example of this fact is provided from the experiences of one of the authors who worked in a program with emotionally disturbed children. Peer tutoring was integrated into the total academic program for the children, who received an average of three and one half hours of classroom instruction per day. Most efforts to match the tutor and tutee were directed at students within the same group level. One teenage girl was in great need of remedial attention in reading and arithmetic. The teacher, seeing an opportunity to involve a boy who had previously remained on the outside of group discussions, asked this boy to work with his classmate in reading thirty minutes a day. The boy, who was of average intelligence and academic ability, was trained in the presentation of materials and reinforcement. The teacher was not aware that a one-to-one situation would be threatening to that girl. She became upset at the mention of working on reading with the tutor, and by the third day of trying, had begun to withdraw from the tutorial situation by not speaking, not looking at the tutor, and exhibiting no overt response to questions by the classroom teacher.

A less dramatic example of an adjustment reaction to the tutorial setting is provided by a teacher who developed and implemented a successful program. Carlos, a third grader in a class that was composed of Mexican-American and black students, was selected to receive tutoring because of his difficulties in mastering the English language. In class, he was seldom in his seat, and according to the teacher, was frequently involved in mischief. A fifth grader, who was a black male, was chosen as his tutor (issues related to the pairing of partners will be discussed later). The tutor was well trained on both the content and procedures of the tutoring process, yet neither he nor the teacher were prepared for the tutee's response to the tutoring situation. Carlos exploded when he was told he was to receive tutoring, and proceeded to frustrate the tutor at every opportunity. He would leap out of his chair, scatter materials, and throw his pencil at the tutor during sessions. The teacher quickly found another tutor for Carlos, but the situation remained the same. Finally, the school psychologist, working with the teacher, developed a behavorial management plan for use in the classroom. When Carlos was better able to monitor his behavior, he was successfully matched with another tutor.

The child who is considered to be very immature may be a poorer risk for a peer tutoring program than a more mature child. The teacher must balance the positive potential for gain by the tutee with the negative potential for an unsuccessful tutorial relationship. In some instances, however, the immature child *can* profit from a tutoring arrangement, especially if the tutor is sensitive to the needs of the partner and can adjust to any behaviors of that child.

The last few paragraphs highlight the importance of the selection decision. It should always be based on a careful consideration of the child's potential to profit from the tutorial relationship, and should reflect the teacher's belief that the learner's behavior can be handled by the tutor without constant supervision. The decision can reflect input from the teacher's personal observation of the child, as well as those of other school personnel and of parents.

The selection procedure can become very involved when the teacher considers all the potential sources of data on a child. The process can be streamlined when several teachers work as a group to evaluate each child, or to create standards or requirements that must be satisfied before a child will be considered for a program. For example, teachers may decide that students may qualify only if they are at least one grade level behind in the tutored subject areas. Or children may be selected from specific grade levels to be tutored.

Programs which contain an extensive research component may apply selection standards which satisfy principles of scientific methodological accuracy, but which make the observer question the validity of the standards. One study, which was conducted using students from the same classroom, chose students to be tutored solely on the basis of one spelling test. Students were divided into tutor and learner groups on the basis of test scores, and were randomly matched into pairs. As a result, a tutor could be paired with a student who on a day-to-day basis received better grades in classroom spelling. However, the structure of the tutorial program was such that this possibility would not affect either the conduct of the tutoring or the potential for learning by the student being tutored.

Following the selection of students to be tutored, the teacher will have in his or her possession data which may have been collected for the post-tutorial evaluation of the student's progress. These data may have been collected prior to the selection decision, and possibly have contributed to the decision, or they may have been collected at any point after selection. The research in most peer tutorial programs evaluates changes from the entry ability or behavioral level of the student to the level of performance on completion of tutoring. There have been few studies which have attempted to collect either process or product data on students during the course of peer tutoring. Such studies have shared, however, one feature of other studies, the pretutorial specification of data collection points. These collection points are usually influenced or determined by the program's research goals and objectives. Chapter 4 discusses in more detail procedures involved in a research component.

In summary, most students exhibit the potential to benefit from being tutored. The child who has severe learning problems or behavioral difficulties can benefit, although greater teacher attention may need to be given to the demands placed on the learner by the tutor. The tutoring studies mentioned throughout this chapter have reported on programs in which students at every grade level, sex, socioeconomic level, and racial/ethnic status have learned within peer tutoring programs. If the child is able and demonstrates a willingness to learn, peer tutoring may be one avenue to provide additional learning experiences.

TUTORS AND THEIR DUTIES

Teachers who are attempting to develop a tutoring program within their own classrooms can usually ask for volunteers to tutor, or they can choose students with particular academic or social-emotional strengths. Guidelines for selecting students to train as tutors vary widely. Teachers may choose any of the following as tutors: (1) students who excel in their school work; (2) students who are well behaved but who have some academic weaknesses; (3) all students who volunteer; or (4) students who meet developed criteria for the tutor role in the program. If the program has been developed to match tutors and learners from the same classroom, the teacher will be able to judge a student's ability to tutor in part by his or her past interactions with peers. A tutor in this context is usually stronger in the academic areas to be taught than is the child to be tutored. In addition, the teacher can choose to focus upon various social skills and emotional strengths of the tutor. A critical portion of the tutor's time will be devoted to creating a supportive atmosphere during the tutoring sessions, providing constructive feedback to the learner, and keeping the learner's attention on the tasks at hand. These responsibilities cannot be taken lightly and still result in the attainment of the goals of the tutorial program.

These considerations also apply to the teacher developing a program of cross-age tutoring. Cohen, Kirk and Dickson (1972) have argued that "much of the effectiveness of the tutoring lies in the personal nature of the interaction." The interaction between an older tutor and a younger learner often is characterized by the unquestioning acceptance of direction by the younger student. The faith placed on the tutor by the tutee is frequently great and in some cases extreme. Consequently, it becomes very important to select tutors who can assume the many responsibilities inherent to the tutor role.

We have discussed the social and emotional responsibilities involved in the tutor role, and which affect to a large extent the effectiveness of the tutor's academically-oriented duties. Tutor duties include not only knowing lesson content, although the training segment of the program can provide the tutor with an adequate background in the subject matter. Other tutor responsibilities, according to Cohen and his colleagues, include having the learner become actively involved in the development of the learning materials. This can be achieved partly by the structured requirements of tutoring sessions, and partly by the tutor's ability to challenge and involve the tutee in the learning process. The tutor, with the contact afforded by the closeness of the learning relationship, can spot academic problem areas of the tutee and focus remedial attention on these deficits. By a process of questioning the learner and asking for responses, the tutor stimulates the learner towards an understanding of appropriate academic and/or social content. Other important tutor skills are listening, prompting, modeling of responses, and reinforcement. In addition, listening or attending skills cannot be taken for granted, especially given the tutor's affective responsibilities in the tutor role. Listening to what the learner is saying may consist of hearing the message's content and secondly the "affect" of the speaker. For example, a child may be giving the correct responses to a series of questions but be speaking in a very nervous and hesitant voice. If attention was directed solely to the content of the child's responses, the tutor would proceed to ask questions at the same rate. When attention is directed to the "tone" of the voice and other affective responses of the learner, the tutor will be able to proceed at a different rate, respond to the affective qualities of the learner's responses, or attempt any of a number of responses to meet the learner's social-emotional needs.

As an example, Stephen was working with a classmate, Bill, on a tutoring program in reading. The teacher, Mrs. Harris, had trained all of the tutors to be aware of the learners' reactions during the daily sessions. Stephen had been taught to ask for Bill's feedback on both the content and process of the tutoring. Stephen had become aware of the importance of watching Bill's nonverbal signals during their meetings. Stephen quickly "knew" when to slow down when Bill seemed to be having trouble learning new materials. He also became aware of the times Bill was becoming restless or bored with the activities. At such times, Stephen would ask Bill if he wanted to go on. If Bill said no, Stephen would close the session with a summary of what had been covered that day. One day, Stephen noticed that Bill was becoming extremely quiet while reading the story in their lesson. The story was about the loss of a pet in a family and how it affected one child. Bill completed his lesson, but clearly appeared to be upset. Gently probing, Stephen discovered that Bill, like the child in the story, had experienced the loss of a pet. By being able to discuss his loss with his tutor, Bill became more open and receptive to Stephen in future sessions. Stephen was seen as a friend, someone to be trusted, and someone who was sensitive to other people's feelings.

Opportunities for expanding the role of the tutor from simply that of a "teacher" are possible, especially if tutorial staff is able to train the tutors in these new role responsibilities. Seldom is it possible to train students for a short period of time in new skills and expect them to succeed in so doing. Even adult teachers require extensive in-service training to acquire similar skills. However, an effective program for training tutors in communication skills, both listening and verbalizing, is possible, given that tutoring staff is specific in just what it expects the tutors to learn. For example, teaching children skills in reflective listening would include teaching students to identify the emotions being expressed by other people. Training could include discussions of the principles of reflective listening, followed by role-playing exercises using this technique. When tutorial dyads are meeting, project staff can observe the sessions, and give feedback to the tutor on the use of the technique. Based on the authors' observations of several programs that have trained tutors on communication skills, successful implementation of new techniques was contingent on the care that was given to the training sessions for the tutors. Well-prepared tutors were more likely than tutors receiving less training to use the techniques appropriately during the tutorial sessions.

Prompting is a skill that enables the tutor to motivate the learner to continue responding and staying on task when the learner seems to be stymied by a particular problem. Modeling of responses is a key not only to the learning and shaping of individual lesson responses but also to the total potential for the tutoring program. The tutor can shape the learner's responses in part by providing examples of correct solutions, such as to a type of math problem. More importantly, the tutor has the skills and the experience that the learner is trying to obtain. The respect that may be given the tutor by the learner reflects, in part, that tutor's ability. Working from such a position of authority, the tutor will be observed in many of his or her actions by the learner and behaviorally modeled. Tutees have been observed to frequently mimic unconsciously the behavior of the tutor during sessions. The tutor needs to be aware of the likelihood that his or her behavior will be copied by the learner, making it important that the actions of the tutor reflect the goals and objectives of the tutorial program.

The tutor, in directing the attention of the learner in the tutorial tasks, can improve both the quantity and quality of the learner's responses by the appropriate and skillful use of reinforcement. The teacher should determine the extent and type of reinforcement, but it is the tutor's task to apply rewards and positive feedback at the correct time and in the proper sequence.

Every student has something to contribute and to gain from his or her experiences as a tutor if proper training, supervision, and follow up is an integral part of the tutorial program's makeup. The teacher, however, needs to be sensitive to the limitations of the students who could qualify to participate in a program. The social-emotional and academic demands placed on the tutor have been discussed above. With these factors as a background, the teacher can assess the student's ability to carry out every demand. Emotional and behavioral inconsistencies may rule out the student who otherwise has the academic credentials to tutor. The immature student, the child who acts out in a destructive manner, the child who seems to disregard the needs of other people, all represent problems which could remove them from consideration for the tutor position. The teacher may determine strengths and needs in these students that will enable them to adjust to the needs of the tutor role and to grow from the experiences. Given the complexity of the selection decision, it is safe to say that if due consideration is not given to this stage of the activities, the program's chances of success are significantly lessened.

Tutoring programs have achieved success using tutors who had their own learning deficiencies. For example, children have been selected as tutors when they were labeled as "learning disabled," but with competencies in one or more basic subject areas. When given the opportunity to assist a younger or "slower" child in an academic or social skill, a learning disabled child will be able to feel a needed sense of success as well as the chance to practice his or her skills in the subject area. Schools utilizing "learning disabled" tutors have reported increased academic and social competencies for both the tutor and the child being tutored.

Selection of tutors usually occurs at the start of the tutorial program. When the need arises, additional tutors can be recruited during the course of the program. As was discussed in the sections on selection of the learner, the teacher's next consideration is to collect all pertinent and required data on the tutors for research and evalution purposes. In pre-post research design, pre-test data collection normally is completed before the tutorial partners ever meet. Several studies have attempted to investigate factors related to the tutor's role in the success of a tutorial relationship. Some factors which have been considered are the sex of the tutor, sex of the partner, age of each participant, intelligence of the tutor, academic ability of the tutor, racial-ethnic characteristics of the partners, and measures of affective characteristics of both dyadic members. These studies can help the teacher in deciding on which students to choose as tutors, and may provide suggestions on additional research questions to investigate through the design of the total program. Given the extent of past research efforts, there is ample opportunity for new and creative investigations into the critical elements of the tutorial arrangement. There are few clear answers on what makes a "good" tutor, what best helps the learner to meet objectives, and other questions regarding the tutorial procedure. The teacher who may, at first, feel unqualified to develop hypotheses for research, collect data, and then analyze it can request assistance from appropriate members of the school district's research and evaluation teams. A sound experimental design which produces accurate results may provide the basis to justify requests for additional grant monies to expand the tutoring program and to investigate factors in peer tutoring more extensively.

In summary, almost every student can potentially serve as a tutor, if given training and supervision that focuses on the specific needs of the learner in the tutoring arrangement. Children with learning problems can help younger children or peers who have fewer academic strengths. The teacher's awareness of the total child is critical in the selection decision. Once children have been selected, the attention of the teacher shifts to training the tutor to maximize his or her own benefits as well as those for the tutee.

TRAINING THE TUTOR

The amount and nature of training for the tutor varies with the teacher, the tutor, and the requirements of the tutoring program. The teacher has to consider time, space, and materials available to devote to training. An additional consideration is whether tutors will be utilized to develop lessons for the program. At the time of selection, the tutor should be acquainted with the goals of the program, as well as the demands which will be placed on the tutor during the course of the program.

The philosophy behind the structure and objectives of a tutorial project may dictate the training program that is presented to the tutors. Some project directors have argued that students tutor best when given minimal training. The belief is based upon the notion that students are natural teachers and are frequently sensitive to the needs of the learner. Other programs have utilized extensive training on both the learning content and the personal-social skills that will be useful to the tutor during teaching sessions. The goals of the training sessions typically include many of the following points (Deterline, 1970):

1 putting the tutee at ease;
2 clarifying the prescribed task;
3 showing the tutee how to verify his or her answer;
4 directing the tutee to read each problem aloud;
5 having the tutee respond overtly, marking or recording responses before the tutor provides feedback;
6 having the tutee verify each response;
7 avoiding any form of punishment;
8 providing verbal praise when appropriate;
9 providing a tangible reward when appropriate; and
10 on designated problems, evaluating all elements of mastery.

An effective training component will emphasize the development of many of these tutor behaviors.

A training program that included these ten steps could involve the following elements:

1 Putting the tutee at ease—emphasize that tutoring can be fun. The tutor should be friendly at all times. "Hi, I'm _____ . What's your name?" "We will be working together for a while, so I'd like to get to know you." Encourage tutors to query their partners about how they are feeling, how their day has been, and so on. This aspect of the tutor/tutee relationship is especially important during the first sessions.

2 Clarifying the prescribed task—typically, a large segment of training sessions for tutors is involved with presenting, in

detail, each step of the tutorial process. Expectations of tutor behavior are defined. For example, often tutors are given time to role-play tutorial sessions, during which careful monitoring of the instructional and social-emotional behavior of the tutor occurs. Feedback to tutors helps them to present themselves and their materials in the manner specified by project staff. A portion of training sessions can be devoted to the task of clarifying the tutorial program for the child being tutored.

3   Showing the tutee how to verify his or her answer—the tutor as manager of the learning situation is expected to show the tutee how to verify a specific answer. First, the tutor must be trained in the expected answers, then in the procedure designated for verifying the response. For example, in one program, the tutor was trained to have the partner compare his or her answer against the answer on a master response sheet. Only then would the tutor provide verbal feedback.

4   Directing the tutee to read each problem aloud—by doing this, the tutor becomes aware of the partner's understanding of the problem. If the partner cannot read the problem out loud, there is little possibility of his knowing what is expected for an answer. Many programs allow the tutor to help the partner read each problem aloud (unless, of course, the program focuses on analysis of reading ability).

5   Having the tutee respond by overtly marking or recording responses before the tutor provides feedback—the tutor, when appropriate, will be trained in the procedures to be followed by the tutee in responding to questions. Training may involve what answer sheets to use and when to use them, as well as how to fill out such sheets. Tutors may be trained additionally in use of other tutorial process forms, such as a tutor log.

6   Having the tutee verify each response—the tutor usually will have the partner compare the correct answer with the answer he or she has given to a question. This step in training tutors is stressed heavily in many tutorial programs that designate a particular manner in which to implement this step.

7   Avoiding any form of punishment—a very important step in training. A large segment of training can be spent profitably

on this point. Train tutors to respond to their partners with "Good, great job, keep it up" when the response is correct, and to remain supportive ("Keep trying, you can do it") when the response is incorrect. At the very least, the tutor should be taught to remain silent, rather than critical, when the partner errs.

8. Providing verbal praise when appropriate—many tutorial projects allow tutors to provide verbal praise whenever the tutor wants to do so. Some projects, however, limit or structure the amount and type of praise to be given. It is helpful to provide tutors with a list of "praise" words and phrases to use during sessions.

9. Providing a tangible reward when appropriate—few tutorial projects provide tangible rewards such as candy or other consumable items, but several do allow tutors to dole out checks, stars, points, or other visible indicators of progress during a session. When such rewards are part of a tutorial program, the tutors will be trained in the appropriate use of them. Such training would involve when to use the rewards and how to present them.

10. On designated problems, evaluating all aspects of mastery—tutors can be trained in what constitutes mastery of a problem, not simply the expected, correct response to a question. During the training phase, project staff will devote time with tutors to explore concepts involved in lessons. With this training, tutors are better prepared to evaluate a tutee's response when it does not match perfectly with the predetermined correct answer.

A Tutor Training Program

The shape and direction taken in tutor training varies with the overall orientation of program planners. Deterline (1970) has extensively outlined a training program that focuses on the active involvement of the tutor in tutoring activities from the beginning of the training sessions. He believes that active involvement is more instructive to the tutor than is listening to lectures on what to do. Introductory comments to tutors may emphasize strategies for helping the learner, but such comments should be kept short.

The following comments summarize aspects of Deterline's approach to tutor training.

First Training Session. In the first training sessions, the teacher demonstrates the differences between the usual teacher-student learning relationship and the tutor-tutee learning relationship. In this fashion, the teacher and assistants can demonstrate the critical behaviors characteristic of the "good" tutor. After these demonstrations, the teacher can discuss with the tutors the tutoring behaviors that had been observed.

A tutoring checklist is then given to the tutors. This checklist contains the behaviors that have been incorporated into the tutor role. It may contain the following behavioral descriptions, which form the basis of Deterline's Tutoring Checklist:

1   The tutor will help the learner to correctly perform tasks that had been performed incorrectly earlier in the lesson. The tutor will do this by asking questions that will focus the learner's attention on the path to the correct answer.

2   The tutor may answer the direct questions of the learner, but the major verbal strategy of the tutor will consist of asking questions of the learner. Feedback and praise necessarily will be declarative statements.

3   Feedback to the learner should be immediate when the learner's response is correct.

4   The tutor will make refined use of the questioning process to assist the learner in the clarification of misunderstood or unknown areas of lesson content.

5   Any errors in response by the learner will result in the tutor asking for a clarification of the response or the procedures which led to that response and will be followed by questions designed to focus the learner on the proper direction to a correct answer.

6   A learner's request for help should trigger a tutor response with the goal of having the learner resolve his or her own difficulties.

7   When the learner says he or she does not understand a question, the tutor will rephrase the question, making it easier to understand and requiring a less involved answer.

8   Demonstrations by the tutor to illustrate learning points should be accompanied by probing the tutee to determine whether the learner is accurately perceiving the demands of the learning tasks.

9   Feedback on correct responses should be given to the learner in a clear and unambiguous manner.

10   While praise should be contingent upon correct responses by the learner, the tutor can provide additional praise for good performance on segments of the exercises.

11   The tutor's behavior always should indicate a positive view of the learner's performance. Negative feedback, whether verbal or facial, has no place in tutoring strategy.

When tutors are given the checklist, it is helpful to demonstrate a tutor-learner session so that the tutor can observe the recommended tutor behaviors. The checklist has additional benefits. Teachers can use it to evaluate the tutor's readiness following a training program and to evaluate the tutor's performance during actual tutorial sessions. Following a demonstration that has been observed by the tutors with their checklist, the teacher should encourage the tutors to describe instances of the performed critical tutor behaviors. The group can critique each other's descriptions of the observed performance. Additional demonstrations can be conducted if the teacher feels that the tutors have not been focusing to a sufficient extent on specific tutor behaviors. Following the second demonstration, the teacher can field questions about the goals of the tutorial project, the level and extent of the tutor's involvement in the project, and any other questions that the tutors may have.

Second Training Session. A second tutor training session attempts to train the students using role play into the tutor role. Tutors will be able to experience both tutor and learner roles in the context of actual tutoring materials. In this way, tutors gain experience with the materials that will be used and become more sensitive to the feelings which the learner may have. The tutor who is playing the learner role can be given cards that will guide his or her responses to tutor prompts. The cards will help both partners to focus on the strategies and verbal responses that are central to the tutor's role. After reviewing each other's performances with the trainer, the partners switch roles. Partners will criticize each other's performance with the teacher. The second session can end with a group discussion of the role playing exercise.

Third Training Session. This session should follow closely after the first two. Sessions should be grouped on consecutive days, if possible, to maximize the learning and memorization of skills by the tutor. The third training session serves to familiarize the tutors with the day-to-day functions expected of them. These functions will have been discussed and structured previously by the teachers in charge of the program.

Tutors can be presented with examples of the materials that will be used in tutorial sessions. All record-keeping forms that must be completed and maintained by the tutor can be explained. The tutors may be given practice sessions in filling out the forms.

Fourth Training Session. This session can be devoted to answering questions about the partners with whom the tutors will be paired. In cross-age tutoring programs, tutors usually have many questions about the age and abilities of their potential partners. The trainer can describe for the tutors recommended social behavior while tutoring. The use of praise and encouragement can be discussed and illustrated with members of the group. A strong emphasis should be placed on maintaining a consistently positive level of exchange with the partner.

Using this training procedure, the teacher has the option of scheduling four sessions of approximately forty-five minutes duration each, or of scheduling shorter and more frequent sessions. Sessions cannot be much longer and still maintain the attention of the tutors. The number and spacing of training sessions usually is contingent on the time and space pressures facing the teacher. The teacher should keep in mind one consideration before making decisions about arranging training sessions—*the more time devoted to training the tutors, the less time will be needed to devote to monitoring and retraining them once the program is in progress.* This factor also applies to other training programs which are described below.

As an interesting aside, Deterline's use of the questioning technique in tutoring differs from that found in most classrooms. Children being tutored are told that the tutor is allowed to ask questions during a session only, not to give the learner direct information.

Responsibility for answering questions rests on the learner. The tutor is trained to help the learner by questioning the partner in his or her responses to the tutorial content. The tutor tells the partner when he or she is correct and praises progress during the sessions. The tutor will not provide answers for the partner. The tutor asks questions to focus the learner on the principles of learning most important to solving a particular problem. To give an example, a child may be asked to give the product of 8×9. If the child answers "48," the tutor may ask, "What is 4×9?" If the child answers correctly, the tutor can proceed to ask progressive products of 9 until the child gives the correct response. The tutor has the freedom of approaching the correct response in other ways, such as reverting to principles of addition to solve a problem in multiplication. Deterline suggests that use of the questioning technique should be stressed in training of the tutors, as consistent use of the technique is quite challenging. Deterline emphasizes the importance of training tutors to give feedback immediately for correct responses. Feedback should clearly be tied to the specific correct response. Praise can be given for more extensive series of correct responses.

Deterline's approach to tutor training is quite structured. The training components reflect his definition of tutorial instruction as interactive instruction. Developing skills in both personal interactions and learning interactions is incorporated into the training process.

Cohen and his colleagues (1972) place similar emphasis on the interactional aspects of the tutoring process. They discuss the importance of skills that engage the learner in the learning process. These skills must be part of any training program that hopes to produce tutors who will be sensitive to the learning and emotional needs of the learner. The tutor is trained to perceive cues that indicate the tutee's engagement in the learning task. Cohen describes four classes of cues: eye, verbal, hand, and posture.

Eye cues are an excellent indicator of agreement. If the learner is looking at the tutor's hands, staring out the window, or sitting with eyes closed, chances are that he or she is not paying much attention to the materials that make up the lesson. If the learner is facially exhibiting interest and enjoyment of the tasks at hand, it is likely that he or she is engaged in the learning task.

Verbal cues also can be a direct indicator of the extent to which the learner is paying attention. If the learner has remained engaged and on task, the learner's responses to questions will reflect the content of the lesson. When the tutee asks a question which does not follow from the materials being discussed, he or she has probably lost track of the learning task. It is especially important for the tutor to pay attention to verbal cues which indicate the learner's fatigue, loss of interest, or affective state. The tutor can intervene to recommend a brief break, end the day's lesson, or deal with the affective components of the learner's responses.

Hand cues similarly can indicate the learner's engagement in the tutorial task. The learner who is writing out answers is likely to be actively involved and on task. The child who is scribbling on the answer sheet or playing with a pencil is likely not to be engaged in the learning task. The tutor can intervene and place learning materials in the tutee's hands.

Posture cues are the final possible indicators of the learner's level of engagement. The reader may be aware of the recent flood of articles and books on "body language." These books are potential sources of information on the various interpretations of body positioning. The child who is slumped over the table or sitting sideways in the chair may be expressing fatigue or lack of interest in the learning process. The tutor can investigate such possibilities by asking the learner whether he or she is tired or wants to take a break. The learner who is sitting up straight and writing down answers to problems is likely to be engaged totally in the learning task.

While the tutor will profit from being trained to be sensitive to cues from the learner, he or she must not be led to believe that there is a hard and fast interpretation for specific learner behaviors. For example, a learner may squirm in his seat while completing math problems. The tutor who interprets the squirming as the learner's discomfort with the learning task may attempt to intervene by taking frequent breaks, thereby lengthening the time spent tutoring. All the learner may be doing is attempting to stay awake after getting little sleep the previous night. The learner otherwise may be attending to the learning task.

Cohen mentions another factor which may influence the interpretation of cues by the tutor. When tutors are expected to work with children of a different racial or ethnic background, learner cues may have different meanings for the child of the minority culture. The teacher who is training the tutors to respond to learner cues will have to train the tutors in the possible different interpretations of cues of engagement and lack of engagement. The tutor may need to be made aware of the behavioral norms of students from particular racial/ethnic backgrounds.

Training attempts to shape tutor behavior so that the tutor creates a learning environment which is nonthreatening to the learner. The tutor can achieve this goal by expressing personal concern for the learner and by reinforcing the correct response of that student. One goal of the tutorial process is to develop self-sufficient learning by the tutee. The child will be taught how as well as what to learn. Questioning, listening, prompting, and modeling of responses are techniques shared by the tutorial programs of Cohen and Deterline. The teacher having similar goals for a tutoring project may choose to incorporate large portions of the training procedures of both authors. Or the teacher may decide to take advantage of elements of local tutoring training projects and incorporate them into the school program's structure.

The Effects of Structure in the Training Process

The extent to which a program is to be structured can affect training activities. For example, a specific technique may be implemented to teach a math concept. It may be important to have the tutors present materials in predetermined sequences and follow specific lesson plans in order to ascertain the effectiveness of the program content.

Structuring the tutorial program so that outcomes can be clearly identified is one feature of the Peer Mediated Instruction (PMI) approach (Rosenbaum, 1973). The PMI approach allows students to work in pairs, with one student designated as the teacher and one as the learner. The "teacher" presents materials such as words from a spelling list to the student, then gives very specific feedback to the student. A correct response receives positive feedback. An incorrect response first involves the "teacher" comparing the student's responses with an answer before beginning the corrective process. Rosenbaum has developed a selective corrective procedure that resembles the partial answer feedback process of IBM computer-assisted-instruction programs. Correction specifies exactly where the error in the response of the learner occurred, then allows repeated attempts by the student to correct the error. Feedback on the correct response to the problem is given so that the student can incorporate partially correct responses in subsequent attempts to solve a problem.

An example will illustrate how the PMI approach can be implemented successfully with students. The PMI approach offers the potential of freeing the classroom teacher from the role of the only instructional leader. The teacher can evolve into a manager of the varied student-teacher dyads working in the classroom on a PMI-styled set of materials. One teacher, Mrs. Adamson, had found that she was devoting more and more time daily to creating materials that challenged students, while not being too difficult to accomplish in a single lesson. Mrs. Adamson's planning period was spent in running off lessons for individual students. When working in the classroom, this teacher felt harried as she went from student to student, attempting to answer their questions and prodding them through their lessons. Hearing of the PMI approach from a colleague, Mrs. Adamson read the Rosenbaum book and was intrigued by the potential application of the PMI system in her class. Mrs. Adamson began by determining the subjects that seemed to require the largest investment of her time in the classroom. Lessons in spelling and reading took the most time for her to gather materials that met her students' academic levels. Mrs. Adamson decided to have the more successful students in these subjects work on the daily lessons with the students who were experiencing difficulty learning the spelling and reading lessons. She continued to use the spelling and reading materials she had used in the past, but trained her "teachers" to employ the PMI approach to giving corrective feedback. Such feedback is always immediate and specific to the error made by the student. Spelling errors received corrective feedback in the manner described previously in the example of Ehly (1975). Reading errors, in this instance the mispronunciation of words, received corrective feedback that was verbal and specific to the point in the pronunciation of the word that the error began. While Mrs. Adamson did not attempt to utilize a more intensive PMI program or to assess the relative efficacy of using this approach above others, she was well pleased with the results. Students liked the learning dyads, and eagerly worked on their lessons with their partners. The PMI approach offers the possibility of "teacher" and learner switching roles, so that both can complete learning materials. This facet of PMI was not implemented in Mrs. Adamson's class. The teacher did find that the PMI approach allowed her greater time to develop new materials for target and other subjects taught in the class.

The study by Ehly (1975) designed a highly successful program to teach spelling to sixth graders using peer tutors from the same classroom. Lesson plans were structured to follow the PMI approach. Early in the program tutors received training in general considerations involved in being a peer tutor, specific procedures required in the PMI tutorial approach to spelling, and practice in role playing as tutor and tutee. An initial hour-long session of training was followed two days later by a refresher course on techniques, with additional practice at role playing. Tutors were given handouts summarizing training session content so that they could study tutoring techniques before the daily tutorial sessions started. A sample of the materials used in the training of tutors for this project is attached as Addendum 3B. These materials may be used as a guide for teachers interested in conducting a similar program. The author scheduled fifteen minutes at the beginning of daily sessions to answer questions from the tutors on the pronunciation and definition of words in each spelling lesson. Tutors were additionally supervised on a day-to-day basis to ensure that they were maintaining standards for the presentation of materials.

Summary on Training

With the many directions that training can take and the number of learner behaviors that a tutor can be taught to interpret and confront, it is helpful to remember Klaus's finding that academic gains for the learner seem to be related to the structure of the tutorial program. The program which very explicitly defines the content, sequence, and procedure of each lesson is more likely to result in learner gains than is the loosely structured program. The most extensively structured program will have little impact if the tutor does not consistently and completely model his or her actions after the tutorial program's model. The training of tutors may not always produce students who will follow strictly the established procedures, but it does help the teacher to determine the likelihood that individual students will meet the behavior expectations attached to the tutor role.

The training component of a tutoring program will reflect the goals and objectives of the total program, whether the objectives are for the individual learner or for overall evaluation of the program's design. Incorporating all the elements of a program into a few training sessions is a task which requires much thought and preparation before a session is held. The teacher who is working with a team of other teachers and school personnel to develop and implement a tutoring project will create a sounder training component if he or she regularly meets with other project staff to discuss goals, designs the procedure for implementing the learning activities to meet these goals, and sequences the steps to instruct tutors in the proper presentation of the learning tasks. The teacher who has selected both tutees and tutors for the program and who has trained the tutors to a predetermined entry level of readiness for tutoring can then begin to pair the students into tutoring dyads.

THE PAIRING PROCESS

The teacher who has extended experience with the children selected to participate in the tutorial program will be able to match children in the tutoring dyads by recognizing the cognitive and affective strengths of the tutor and the needs of the learner. Pairs which do not seem to be working well together can be reassigned to new partners. The requirements of the tutorial program and the goals which have been created for the tutor and learner can influence the pairing decision.

One area of the program that may affect the pairing decision is the evaluation component. Evaluation needs may require a specific method of pairing tutor and learner. For example, tutors and tutees may be assigned to pairs using a random assignment procedure. This procedure, which has a basis in statistical theory, seemingly does not take into account the individual differences and needs of the tutor and learner. However, it may ensure that the results obtained in the analysis of project data do not reflect situational factors and artifacts.

The student who has been trained to be sensitive to the many needs of the learner may be an effective and productive tutor with any child. The teacher will balance considerations of potential tutor effectiveness with the needs of the program. A cross-age tutorial program, with its emphasis on working with younger children, introduces the need to match the better trained and more sensitive tutors with the more immature of the tutee group. The teacher working with a peer-tutoring program within a single classroom or group of classrooms at the same grade level must attend to existing relationships that could interfere with the progress of daily sessions. Especially in such programs, consideration must be given to differences in peer status and liking that could cause conflicts within the closeness of the tutoring sessions. Of course, if the teacher's goals include improving the relationships of particular students in the class, the program can be structured to achieve this goal.

While few tutoring dyads do not succeed, on occasion the removal of the tutor from the entire program may be necessary. It is a good policy to monitor the pairs closely, particularly at the beginning of the program, and to make reassignments when learning and affective goals are not being met or procedures are not being followed. There are several possible reasons why a pair may not work well together. Personality differences may evolve and lead to uncooperativeness by the learner and even active sabotaging of assignments. Siblings usually make poor pairs, given the likelihood of conflict existing between them. Deterline (1970) states that brighter students should be paired to brighter learners, and less bright tutors to less bright learners. This, however, is by no means a recommended procedure, especially when you are working in a cross-age tutoring program.

Some tutorial project managers believe that boy tutors should be matched with boy learners, and girl tutors matched with girl learners. The argument is that the boys work better with boys, and the girls better with other girls. Dahlen (1973) conducted a study in which high school students tutored third graders. Following a program of tutoring to meet reading objectives, he found that tutors of the same sex as the learners had a greater influence on the outcome scores of the learners in reading. Children with same-sex tutors scored higher on posttests in reading than did the children in cross-sex pairs. A similar effect was not found for tutoring in arithmetic. Apparently the sex of the tutorial partner may be related to learner outcomes under certain conditions.

Ehly (1975) investigated as part of a larger project the effects of same-sex and opposite-sex pairings on the learning outcomes for students in a tutorial program in spelling. There was no difference on learning outcomes between the pairing arrangements. One finding of interest was that learners in same-sex pairs liked their partners more following tutoring than was true of the learners in opposite-sex pairs.

Teachers may be uncertain about matching students with differing racial or ethnic backgrounds. A few studies of the effects of same racial/ethnic grouping versus different racial/ethnic grouping have not provided a definite answer to questions about the differing arrangements. Dahlen (1973) in a cross-age tutorial program using high school and college tutors working with third graders investigated the effects of matching Chicano students with either Chicano or Anglo tutors on reading performance. He found that Chicano children did not perform significantly better for Chicano tutors than for Anglo tutors. In light of the equivocal nature of available data, teachers will need to consider each tutorial pair to determine the potential effects of racial or ethnic differences.

A useful instrument that can be used by the teacher to help make the pairing decision is a "liking" scale (see Addendum 4A for an example of such a scale). Children can be asked to rank-order, in terms of liking, other students in the class. With this information from both tutors and tutees, the teacher can match students that like each other to roughly the same degree. There are many sociometric instruments that can provide similar information, but phrased in terms such as the extent to which a child would like to play with another child. These instruments can be very useful to the teacher who needs information on which to base selection and pairing decisions. They can be incorporated into the evaluation design to investigate changes in the participants' feelings and perceptions over the course of the tutorial program.

The pairing decision can be made best when guidelines have been established for making that decision. The optimal time to sit down with other project members and discuss this issue is before the participants are selected. As noted, decisions may follow from evaluation needs, or they may take into account a range of other alternative options. While pairings need not be permanent, the need for reassignments during the course of the program will decrease with the amount of care given to planning at this stage in the overall program.

Selecting Aides for a Tutorial Program

Not all students in a classroom may work in a tutoring program, but it is a sure bet that most children will want to be involved in some way. Given the many forms that may need to be completed during and after each session and the need to monitor the length of sessions, students can be selected to fulfill these tasks. The aide role carries with it as many responsibilities as there are needs for data collection, distribution of papers and forms, and other maintenance tasks. When the teacher has eliminated students from consideration as tutors because of lack of openings or because of some academic or affective/behavioral factor, the aide position can serve to involve students in the ongoing program in the classroom. While goals for these children need not be defined as was so for tutors and learners, the teacher can help a student assume a role of responsibility as an aide.

In one tutoring project, students were divided into pairs on the basis of scores on a pretest. To establish experimental control for research purposes, children who were bilingual were not assigned to tutor or learner groups. These students eagerly sought out positions as aides in the project, and did an excellent job of passing out data forms and timing the length of each session, both tasks being evaluation requirements. The aide position will be valued by the student if the teacher emphasizes the importance of the role and its duties. The teacher may want to monitor the performance of students in these tasks, if only to insure that data are being collected as scheduled.

Tutoring Across Racial and Ethnic Groups

This topic has been mentioned as a potential consideration in the selection and pairing of students. Cohen, Kirk and Dirkson (1972) have discussed several guidelines that can become part of a total program. The authors suggest that:

1 the tutor should not pry into the family life or lifestyle of the minority group learner, but let that student initiate such discussions;
2 the tutor should not attempt to act as an expert on the culture of the minority child;

3   the tutor must avoid any criticism or copying of the learner's speech patterns and dialect;

4   the tutor should be sensitive to his or her own socioeconomic status and the effects, if any, of this status and its attendant values on the learner;

5   the tutor should focus on establishing and maintaining a skill-oriented relationship which can be enjoyed by the learner;

6   the selection of a space for tutoring should take into account both the needs for an undisturbed working area and the feelings of the learner who may be embarrassed to be tutored in front of others; and

7   the tutor must go more than halfway to meet the needs of the learner.

These guidelines for working with students from minority groups can be included in the training procedures for tutors and influence the teacher's decision in the selection of tutors who can best meet these specifications. Again, consideration given to these factors in a cross-racial or ethnic group tutorial program can lessen the possibility of adjustment difficulties between partners later in the program. The well-trained and affectively-skilled tutor will be better able than a less-skilled tutor to achieve the objectives of any tutorial program.

Addendum 3A
SAMPLE TUTORIAL OBJECTIVES

Subject: *Reading*
Level: *Primary*

General Objective

The student uses initial consonant sounds to decode unfamiliar words.

Specific Objectives

1 Given a series of letters, the student names the letter and gives its sound.
2 Given a series of words which begin with a consonant letter, the student names the initial consonant.
3 Given a series of familiar words, the student names the initial consonant and its sound.
4 Given a series of letters, the student names words from his/her reading vocabulary that begin with that consonant.
5 When given a consonant letter to be placed at the beginning of familiar phonetic patterns, such as *at, an, in,* the student correctly reads the newly formed word aloud.

b <u>at</u>	f <u>an</u>	b <u>in</u>
c <u>at</u>		t <u>in</u>

Subject: *Reading*
Level: *Elementary*

General Objective

The student comprehends material that he/she reads silently.

Specific Objectives

1 After reading a series of paragraphs silently, the student orally states the main idea of each paragraph.
2 After reading a short story silently, the student lists the characters in the story.
3 After reading a page silently from the basal reader, the student orally retells in his/her own words what has been read.
4 After reading a story silently, the student discusses the main events of the story.
5 When given the main events from a story that the student has read silently, the student arranges the events in the order that they occurred in the story.

Subject: *Reading*
Level: *Secondary*

General Objective

The student analyzes words into their basic structural parts, i.e., prefix, root word, suffix.

Specific Objectives

1 The student chooses from a list of prefixes and suffixes.
2 Given a set of root words, the student attaches a suffix to each root word.

care + ful = careful
help + ful = helpful

3 Given a set of root words, the student attaches a prefix to each root word.

re + write = rewrite
re + read = reread

4 Given a list of words containing either a prefix or a suffix, the student circles the prefix or suffix and notes whether the circled part is a prefix or suffix.

un kind = prefix   forget ful = suffix

5 Given a list of words containing a prefix, a suffix or both, the student circles the root word.

dis content   re state   un happi ness

Subject:	*Written Expression*
Level:	*Primary*

General Objective

The student demonstrates the use of capitalization rules in his/her written work.

Specific Objectives

1 When copying a sentence from the board, the student begins each sentence with a capital letter.
2 Given a series of words, the student copies the words and places a capital letter at the beginning of each word that is a person's name.
3 Given a set of sentences, the student places a star by each sentence that begins with a capital letter.
4 Given a set of sentences, the student places a star by every name that begins with a capital letter.
5 The student writes three original sentences and uses correct capitalization at the beginning of each sentence and every name.

Subject: *Written Expression*
Level: *Elementary*

General Objective

The student knows the four types of sentences—declarative, interrogative, exclamatory and imperative.

Specific Objectives

1 The student names the four types of sentences and orally defines each type.
2 The student lists the four types of sentences and gives one example of each type.
3 Given a set of sentences, the student identifies the type of each sentence.
4 The student makes a chart showing the four types of sentences and their end punctuation.
5 Given a set of sentences, the student places the correct punctuation mark at the end of each sentence.

Subject: *Written Expression*
Level: *Secondary*

General Objective

The student demonstrates skills in written expression through letter writing.

Specific Objectives

1 The student lists the five main parts of an informal letter.
2 Given a model of a letter written to a friend, the student labels each main part of the letter.
3 The student cites examples of five different closings that could be used when writing to a friend.
4 Given a model of an informal letter, the student supplies the necessary capital letters in the heading, greeting, closing and signature.
5 Given a model of an informal letter, the student punctuates the greeting and closing.
6 The student writes a letter to a friend that contains the five main parts of a letter with correct punctuation and capital letters.

Subject: *Spelling*
Level: *Primary*

General Objective

The student demonstrates awareness of letter sounds in spelling unfamiliar words with a consonant-vowel-consonant pattern.

Specific Objectives

1 Given a worksheet consisting of pictures of familiar objects, the student identifies the initial sound of each word.
2 Given a set of words, the student identifies the ending sound of each word.
3 When words are orally presented, the student identifies the number of sounds in each word.
4 Given a set of pictures symbolizing one-syllable words with a short vowel in the medial position, the student lists the vowel for each picture.
5 When orally presented words with a consonant-vowel-consonant pattern, the student writes each word.

Subject: *Spelling*
Level: *Elementary*

General Objective

The student demonstrates awareness of homonyms.

Specific Objectives

1 The student defines the term "homonym."
2 The student compiles a list of frequently used homonyms.
3 Given ten pairs of homonyms, the student writes a sentence using each homonym.
4 Given a set of sentences containing a homonym in each sentence, the student circles the proper homonym for that picture. Example: We (ate eight) pancakes this morning.
5 When orally presented a homonym and a sentence using the homonym, the student gives the correct spelling for the homonym.

Subject: *Spelling*
Level: *Secondary*

General Objective

The student demonstrates accuracy in spelling commonly used words.

Specific Objectives

1 The student lists fifteen words that he/she has difficulty spelling.
2 The student devises a sentence using each word.
3 The student divides each spelling word into syllables.
4 The student analyses each word for prefixes, suffixes, etc.
5 The student spells each word as it is dictated by the tutor.

Subject: *Social Studies*
Level: *Primary*

General Objective

The student comprehends the role of community helpers.

Specific Objectives

1 After viewing a film over community helpers, the student names various community helpers.
2 When shown pictures of different community helpers, the student describes the job that each community helper performs.
3 The student makes a chart related to community helpers that contains pictures and a one-sentence job description.
4 The student matches pictures of community helpers with the materials that are associated with their jobs.
5 The student presents an oral report consisting of at least five sentences regarding a community helper in his/her city.

Subject: *Social Studies*
Level: *Elementary*

General Objective

The student demonstrates awareness of the problems of drug abuse.

Specific Objectives

1 After reading a chapter concerning drug abuse in the basal social studies text, the student defines frequently used vocabulary associated with the area of drug abuse. Examples: withdrawal, addiction, dosage, hallucinogenic, narcotics.
2 The student collects five articles from newspapers, magazines, etc., concerned with drug usage.
3 The student constructs a chart listing drugs that are commonly found in the home.
4 After viewing a film on drug addiction, the student discusses the main ideas presented in the film.
5 The student compiles a notebook containing basic information regarding various types of drugs, such as their classification, effects and availability.

Subject: *Social Studies*
Level: *Secondary*

General Objective

The student interprets a weather map.

Specific Objectives

1 The student charts the typical weather for each season of the year in his/her city.
2 The student views the weather forecast on television for five evenings and orally reports on the forecast the following day.
3 When presented with a worksheet consisting of the symbols that are used on a weather map, the student identifies the symbols.
4 Given a weather map of the U.S., the student orally reports the weather conditions in an area that is chosen by the tutor.
5 The student constructs a weather map of the United States which includes five different weather symbols.

Subject: *Math*
Level: *Primary*

General Objective

The student knows the basic addition facts for whole numbers with sums from 1–20.

Specific Objectives

1 When shown a whole number from 1–20, the student states the name of the numeral, e.g., $15 =$ _____ , $9 =$ _____ , $2 =$ _____ .

2 When given the name of a whole number from 1–20, the student will write the corresponding symbol for the numeral, e.g., five = _____ , seven = _____ , eleven = _____ .

3 When presented flashcards of basic addition problems with whole number sums from 1–20, the student states the answer to each problem, e.g.,

$$\begin{array}{cccc} 5 & 7 & 2 & 4 \\ +6 & +8 & +1 & +6 \\ \hline \end{array}$$

4 Given a worksheet consisting of basic addition problems with whole number sums from 1–20, the student supplies the answer to each problem, e.g.,

$$5 + 7 = \qquad \begin{array}{c} 8 \\ +4 \\ \hline \end{array} \quad \begin{array}{c} 11 \\ +1 \\ \hline \end{array} \qquad 12 + 3 =$$

5 Given a whole number sum from 1–20, the student lists three pairs of whole number addends that will give that sum.

$12 =$ _____ $+$ _____ $9 =$ _____ $+$ _____

$12 =$ _____ $+$ _____ $9 =$ _____ $+$ _____

$12 =$ _____ $+$ _____ $9 =$ _____ $+$ _____

Subject: *Math*
Level: *Elementary*

General Objective

The student knows the process of adding fractions.

Specific Objectives

1 When presented with a fraction, the student states the numeral in the numerator and in the denominator.

$$\frac{7}{8}$$ - numerator, denominator $$\frac{9}{10}$$ - numerator, denominator

2 When presented with equations containing fractional addends with like denominators, the student writes the sum for each fraction.

$$\frac{1}{5} + \frac{3}{5} = \qquad \frac{6}{8} + \frac{1}{8} = \qquad \frac{4}{7} + \frac{2}{7} =$$

3 When presented pairs of numerals, the student lists a common multiple for the pairs.

$$(4, 8) \underline{\hspace{1cm}} \qquad (5, 7) \underline{\hspace{1cm}} \qquad (2, 3) \underline{\hspace{1cm}}$$

4 When presented with fractions, the student renames each fraction by reducing it to its lowest form.

$$\frac{4}{8} = \qquad \frac{3}{6} = \qquad \frac{4}{12} =$$

5 When presented with equations containing fractional addends with unlike denominators, the student writes the sum for each fraction.

$$\frac{1}{2} + \frac{5}{6} = \qquad \frac{2}{3} + \frac{4}{5} =$$

Subject: *Math*
Level: *Secondary*

General Objective

The student knows the computational steps required for the addition of decimals.

Specific Objectives

1 When presented with fractions with denominators of ten, the student renames the fractions as decimal numerals.

$$\frac{1}{10} = \qquad \frac{7}{10} =$$

2 When presented with fractions with denominators of 100, the student renames the fractions as decimal numerals.

$$\frac{2}{100} = \qquad \frac{15}{100} =$$

3 When presented with decimals expressed to the tenths place, the student writes the equivalent fractions.

$$\frac{7}{10} = \qquad \frac{8}{10} =$$

4 When presented with decimals expressed to the hundredths place, the student writes the equivalent fractions.

$$\frac{16}{100} = \qquad \frac{25}{100} =$$

5 When presented with equations containing two decimal addends expressed to the tenths or hundredths place, the student finds the sums.

$$\begin{array}{r} 2.1 \\ +5.6 \\ \hline \end{array} \qquad \begin{array}{r} 1.75 \\ +2.13 \\ \hline \end{array}$$

Subject: *Class Behavior*
Level: *Elementary*

General Objective

The student completes math assignments independently within the designated class time.

Specific Objectives

1 The student completes five math problems during the tutoring session with the tutor's help.
2 Given five math problems, the student works three without the tutor's help.
3 Given five math problems, the student works each problem independently while the tutor stays with the student.
4 The student completes two math problems independently at his/her desk while the tutor helps another student.
5 The student completes five math problems independently within fifteen minutes while sitting at his/her desk.

Addendum 3B
SAMPLE TUTOR HANDOUTS AND STUDY MATERIALS

Things to remember—

Smile. Be friendly at all times.

Ask your partner friendly questions before each session.

Have your partner write down each word as you say it.

Praise your partner when he or she spells a word correctly. Never criticize your partner.

If an answer is not correct, work with your partner until he or she spells the word correctly.

Here is the first tutoring technique you will need to know.

Do things that will put your partner at ease.

The first thing you will do when you meet your partner is to ask friendly questions and do things that will make him or her feel comfortable with you.

When you ask your partner questions, smile and speak in a friendly voice. Be careful not to speak too fast.

Remember: Be friendly and kind.
             Never say "that's wrong" or "no."
             Never say or do anything that will make your partner feel bad.

It is important that you read over the spelling words and sentences before you start with the day's session. If you do not know how to pronounce a word or know the word's meaning, talk with your training leader before the session. Fifteen minutes will be provided for this.

At the beginning of a day's session, fill out your name, your student's name, and the date on the top of the lesson sheet and answer sheet.

It is important that your student spell out loud each word and then write it on the answer sheet as you present it. Be sure at the beginning of each session that your student knows that he or she must write down the spelling.

Now you are ready to start teaching.

For each daily session, you must follow the procedures listed below: Look over the lesson sheet for the day. There will be ten words to cover in the session. The sheet will have the same format every day.

Important—things you can say to praise your student:
  Very good.
    Very, very good.
      You are really doing well.
        You really know how to spell.
          That's right.

Try thinking of other ways to praise your student, so that you don't always say the same thing.

Say things that will make your student feel that he or she is doing well so that he or she will enjoy being tutored.

When you praise your student, speak clearly, and say it so that you sound pleased.

If the student does not spell a word correctly, do not say things like:
  You are wrong.
  Oh, no!
  Why did you do that?

You must always remember to sound positive. Emphasize exactly where the error is in the spelling, and that the student will be allowed to try to spell the word until he or she gets it correct.

If you do not remember how to show the student that an answer is incorrect, just follow the earlier directions on what to say and do in correcting a word.

Notes from the training sessions:

Here is a sample item from a lesson sheet:
  Grain   We gathered the grain in the field.   Grain

Your task is to read slowly and clearly
  "Grain.   We gathered the grain in the field.   Grain".

You may repeat the entire sequence if the student asks you to do so.

Tell the student to write down the spelling of the word you present (in the sample case, the word "grain") onto the first section of the first line of the answer sheet.

If the student spells the word correctly, say "that's right," or "very good." Then go to the next word in the lesson.

But what if the student's answer is not right? You will point to the student's answer and say:

"Everything you have written to the left of the vertical slash (you will put in the slash) is correct, but everything to the right of that slash is an error."

Here's how you put in the slash.

If the correct spelling of the word is	grain
and the student writes down	grane

you put in the slash like this:	gra/ne.

Then you say, "Try spelling the word 'grain' again."

The student will write down his second attempt at spelling the word in the second section of the line for that word, here "grain." If the student spells the word correctly, say "that's right" and go on to the next word of the lesson. If the student does not spell the word correctly, put a vertical slash at the point where the student made his error.

If the word to spell is	grain
and the student, on the second try, spells	graim

you put in the slash	grai/m.

Tell the student that everything to the right of the slash is an error and try to spell the word. If the student wants you to give the word in the sample sentence again, you may repeat the original sentence.

The student will write down the third attempt at spelling the word in the third section of the line for that word. If the student spells the word correctly, say "that's right" and go on to the next word in the lesson.

If the student does not spell the word correctly on the third attempt, show him or her the correct spelling. Write out the word on your scratch paper and let the student look at it. Tell the student, "we will be returning to this word in a little while, so you will get another chance to spell it correctly."

Go through the ten words in the daily lesson in the order that they are on the lesson sheet and follow the same procedures listed above.

After your have gone through the list once, allowing for up to three attempts at spelling a word correctly, you will have completed the first cycle of presentation. You are then to go back to those words that were missed by your student in the first cycle.

You will say to the student, "We are going to try to spell again the words that you have missed." In re-presenting the words, read each one in the same manner used on the lesson sheet.

For example, if the student incorrectly spelled the word "grain" on the third attempt in the first cycle, you would say,

"Grain. We gathered the grain in the field. Grain."

The student will write down the spelling of the word in the fourth segment of the line for that word. If the student spells the word correctly, say "that's right," or "good," or something else positive.

If the student spells the word incorrectly, follow the same procedures you used in the first cycle. Say "I am placing this slash, so that everything to the right of it is what you will need to change to spell the word correctly." Tell the student to spell the word again.

Following the same procedures, give the student a total of three tries at spelling the word correctly in the second cycle. If the student does not spell the word correctly by the third try, show him or her again the correct spelling, and say that you will return to that word later.

If any words are not spelled correctly by the third attempt of the cycle, you will follow the same procedures in presenting the words for as many trials as are necessary for the student to spell the word correctly. The format of presentation will continue to be:

Present   word-sample sentence-word.

Praise   if the spelling is correct.

Correct   with a slash when the spelling is incorrect.

Allow   up to three attempts per cycle at spelling a word before you show the correct spelling.

Here is the way that an answer sheet could look after a session.

SAMPLE ANSWER SHEET

1 Grain
2 Far/ner   Farmer
3 Barnyard
4 Tr/ectre   Tract/re   Tractor
5 Chores
6 Midwife
7 Shep/erd   She/eperd   Shep/ard   Sheph/ard   Shepherd
8 Ranch
9 Cowboy
10 Whe/et   Wheat

When all the words on a lesson sheet have been correctly spelled at least once by your student, add up the number of trials per word and record on the lesson sheet. Then turn in your lesson sheet and answer sheet to the aide.

You will then start working on SRA materials.

Notes to the Tutor

Lessons are planned so that you should take about thirty minutes to complete the materials. If more time is needed, you may take longer.

If the student does not get the first letter of a word correct, help him or her to sound out the letter.

Your tutor log is to be filled out daily and turned in at the end of the week. Make sure to make note of the time you met with the student on a day. Just write down the time you started the session and the time you ended. Be sure to write down whether you were meeting for a regular or a makeup session. Also put down any comments about the student that seem important to you.

You must remember to praise the student every time he or she gives the correct spelling of a word.

4
STRUCTURING A PEER TUTORING PROGRAM

Previous chapters have explored procedures in selecting and training students for a peer tutoring program. The procedures discussed suggested several methods of selecting students, training them, and pairing them to work with each other. These procedures, however, are not enough to insure success when schools first establish a peer tutoring program. The intent of this chapter is to explore the structure in a tutorial program, and how attention to the components of structure can determine, to a large part, whether or not a particular project will be successful.

Just as the integrity and strength of the pieces of a chair work in a particular arrangement to achieve the overall soundness of that chair, so do the several elements of the tutorial program and their arrangement combine to create the outcomes desired for the student participants. Each element must be developed so as to insure the functional utility of that component, and then be fitted into the total program at an optimal time to achieve optimal results. Considerations of the structure of a tutorial program may focus on the *physical arrangements* (e.g., the placement of tutorial dyads into work areas and the orientation of tutor to tutee once seated), *temporal factors* (e.g., length of training sessions, length of individual sessions, length of total program), *scheduling requirements* (emphasis on consistency of arrangements), *monitoring and evaluation components*, and other factors such as the integration of tutorial content with these structural factors.

EXAMPLES OF TUTORIAL PROGRAMS

Before considering the many factors that are involved in decisions on the structure of a tutorial project, let us consider two tutorial programs and the manner in which they were carried out. The purpose for discussing these tutorial programs is to highlight the critical importance of structural considerations in establishing a tutorial program. One tutorial program was very successful—structure was specific and well-monitored. The second program was less than successful as a result of the teacher's devoting less time to aspects which related directly to managerial concerns.

A Structured Tutorial Program

The goal of the first program was that students being tutored would learn 200 previously unknown words from a spelling list. Each session was approximately 30 minutes long and consisted of teaching 10 words. There were a total of 20 sessions in the four-week program. Tutors were encouraged to try to finish each session with the partner within 30 minutes, although somewhat later finishing times were permitted. The thirty-minute span was designed to meet the scheduling needs of the teacher and to be short enough so that the children would be able to stay on task during the entire session.

Tutorial procedures followed the guidelines of the Peer Mediated Instruction approach suggested by Rosenbaum (1973) and the individualization approach of Rowell (1972). Tutor guidelines for the presentation of the materials were included in the tutor study materials that were a segment of the tutor training process. These materials are included in Addendum 3B to Chapter 3.

Tutoring sessions were held in two large classrooms. Each tutoring session progressed as follows. (1) Tutors wrote down their names and the names of their partners on several forms—Tutor Logs, Lesson Sheets, and the Daily Answer Sheet for the tutee (these forms may be found on pages 128–130 in Addendum IV-A). (2) The Lesson

Sheet contained the daily group of 10 words to spell as well as the sentences containing the target word. (3) Tutors would say the first word, give the sentence containing the word, and then repeat the word. Tutors were allowed to repeat words and sample sentences upon request by the tutee. (4) The tutee wrote down the spelling of each word in the first word space on the Answer Sheet. (5) The tutor responded with praise when the answer was correct, and then went on to the next word in the lesson. (6) When the answer was incorrect (that is, the word was misspelled), the tutor drew a vertical slash at the point where the tutee's spelling error began. The tutor said, "Everything you have written to the left of the vertical slash is correct, but somewhere to the right of that slash there is an error." The student was then encouraged to spell the word again. If he or she could spell the word correctly, praise was given and then the student proceeded to the next word on the daily list. If the student misspelled the word again, the same process was followed placing the slash at the point of error and then allowing for another trial. If the student succeeded on the third trial, he or she proceeded to the next word on the daily list. If the student failed on the third attempt, the tutor would write the correct spelling of the word on a sheet of scratch paper and tell the student that he or she would get a chance at spelling that word later in the session.

The tutor proceeded through the 10-word daily list until every word had been tried with a maximum of three attempts. Words missed on the third attempt were recycled to a second list. Up to three trials were allowed per word in a second cycle through the list. If the student missed the spelling of a word on the third trial of the second cycle, this word was again recycled, after the correct spelling was shown with other words missed. Subsequent cycles contained the same format of presentation of words and feedback processes for correct and incorrect responses, until all words were spelled correctly once. (7) Tutee attempts at spelling each word on any trial and cycle were recorded by the tutee in the appropriate spaces on the answer sheet. (8) When the spelling list had been completed for the day, the tutor took the Lesson Sheet and Answer Sheet to the tutoring supervisor. This person recorded the time of completion of the session and calculated the length of the session. If the tutoring pair finished before the thirty-minute mark of the session, it were given traditional seat work activities. Tutor Logs were completed and submitted by the tutors on a weekly basis.

The students were tested according to prespecified procedures at a date following within three days of the completion of the tutoring program. A posttest was given to all experimental subjects (i.e., tutors and their partners) on the 200 words of the tutoring sessions' content. The posttest examiners were the regular classroom teachers who had administered the spelling pretest. A test of the generalization of learning in spelling also was given to the tutees. This 100-word list was used to assess generalization of the motivation to spell rather than the generalization of specific spelling techniques.

A "perceived affect" rating scale and a "perceived competency" rating scale were administered to the tutors and their partners. Each tutor rated his or her partner's affect and competency during the tutoring sessions. The children being tutored rated the tutor's affect and competency as displayed during the tutorial sessions. "Perceived affect" and "perceived competency" rating scales can be found in Addendum 4B.

Tutors and their partners had previously rank-ordered, in terms of liking, five students in the class. Unknown to them at the time, their potential tutorial partner was one of the five names. In the posttests, tutors and tutees were presented the same five names to rank-order in terms of liking. A directional score then could be calculated of liking for the partner. (A sample of the liking form can be found in Addendum 4B).

The Tutor Logs and Answer Sheets contained references to the length of each tutoring session by a tutoring dyad. A coefficient for each dyad over the twenty sessions was used to indicate tutoring pair, defined as the number of words per session divided by the average length, in minutes, of the sessions. The mean coefficient for each dyad over the twenty sessions was used to indicate the learning efficiency of the tutorial pair.

The tutorial project was successful in that the tutees learned more than half of the spelling words by the end of the brief program. Students matched in tutorial pairs liked each other more by the end of the sessions. Teachers reported that students who had participated in the project worked more closely and more frequently with each other in the regular classroom. Tutorial programs that are designed with care and are closely monitored can result in significant affective and learning gains for tutors and tutees.

An Unstructured Tutorial Program

A tutorial program that differed in many ways from the above research-oriented project was conducted in a large Southwestern middle school. A sixth-grade teacher and an eighth-grade teacher had discussed on many occasions the need for a cooperative tutoring program using their respective students, but space and time seemed too limited. A colleague agreed to help the two teachers to search out an optimal space arrangement if they would work on scheduling times for tutoring pairs to meet. As a result of the fact that the students participating in the program were few in number, the teachers decided to have those who volunteered for the project meet during a morning break. The small number of students involved in the program enabled the scheduling of resource room space and library space for the duration of the tutoring. The teachers did not require the students to meet regularly. The tutors were provided packets of materials to cover when they met in a session with the partner. Tutoring dyads met until a student did not want to continue or until the teacher found other uses for a student's time. Teachers noted that little was learned in these sessions, although the children reported to the teachers that they enjoyed working with their partners. The students' response caused the teachers to reassess the structure of their program, and to attempt to implement a tutorial design that could achieve better academic results for the students.

The two peer tutorial programs outlined above differed in many ways, primarily in their structure and differing outcomes. One program trained the tutors, while the other did not. Both programs had the pairs meet in particular rooms, but the programs were not similar in the consistency with which students met their partners. In both instances, pairs met during free times, or times that could readily be changed to a free-time status; and both programs provided the tutors with materials to use with the partner, although the research-based program defined in very specific terms the nature of the presentation of materials. Time limits were (loosely) applied in one program, while in the other the students were free to terminate a session at any time. In the research-based program, session length was influenced also by the difficulty of lesson content. Other differences between these and similar programs will highlight some of the choices that teachers have in creating their tutorial program.

STRUCTURAL CONSIDERATIONS WHEN ESTABLISHING A PEER TUTORING PROGRAM

Of immediate importance at the beginning of any tutoring program is soliciting the active support of the school principal and other administrators. These people usually control access in the school to both space and materials. In many buildings the principal requires (for a number of reasons) notification of special projects. It may be mandatory to notify the principal before any research design is put into operation. Research that attempts to meet the ethical standards of an educational organization must be approved by the parent or guardian of any student that participates in the study. This permission should be in writing, and should specify exactly what will be done with the child, what data will be collected, and how these data will be used. Confidentiality must be guaranteed to all children who participate in the research effort. The principal or other school administrators can inform the staff of the school district's policies regarding research in the schools. Teachers may even have access to the district's research department, and possibly receive assistance in evaluating the tutorial program.

Discussion beyond the introduction of a program's goals with the principal may focus on the availability of space and materials. Of course, the scope of a program will directly affect staff demands on space and materials additional to those already available in the classrooms of participating teachers. The principal and teachers may be able to negotiate an agreement whereby program needs for additional space and materials will be met when the success of a pilot program has been demonstrated to the principal. While participating teachers may prefer immediate access to the needed space and materials, the concept of a pilot program is a sound one, especially when the major goal of a program is to generate data to test research hypotheses. The pilot effort can serve to give teachers time to ensure that research measures are doing what teachers want them to do—measure a particular factor or strategy. During the pilot program, it is possible to assess the efficacy of tutor training program components, or to see if the project's materials can be readily used by tutors and understood by their partners. The time devoted to this pre-project level can be well spent in terms of producing the outcomes desirable in the actual program effort.

The small or beginning tutorial program can be conducted in a variety of settings. Cohen et al. (1972) state that tutors should work in a setting where there are few, if any, distractions to impinge on the awareness of the partners. The teacher will be looking first for the best possible space arrangement for the group of students. Once tutoring has started, the individual pairs may be unable to work in a particular location. For example, a room may be too noisy for a particular student to work, or a different student may associate placement in a specific room with negative connotations (e.g., time-out room). The tutoring room may be seen as a place where students go when they have exhibited noticeable learning problems. At this point the teacher has the choice, if necessary, of intervening with the student to attenuate these feelings or placing the student in another area appropriate for peer tutoring. One way of structuring the tutorial context is to have several spaces in which the pairs can meet. Students may be assigned these spaces or may be free to choose the "niche" that suits them best.

Because of space limitations, the teacher may desire to have the pairs meet in the same classroom at the same time. A potential limitation in this arrangement (other than the noise) is that the child being tutored or the tutor may feel self-conscious working on the tutorial task. In the authors' opinion, children tend to be extremely self-conscious when they are matched with a partner whom they perceive to have low group status. This is more likely to occur when the students differ widely in peer group acceptance, although liking of the students for each other can negate such a consequence. A variation of the preliminary discomfort felt by partners in a tutorial context has been seen frequently in the lower to middle grades. This occurs when pairs are matched in boy-girl dyads. In one study with sixth graders, the children moaned and groaned about being placed with a member of the opposite sex.

Fortunately, the complaints soon subsided and the children got down to work. Initial hesitancies can be worked out with continued contact between the children. The teacher must remain sensitive to the length of the adjustment period. As discussed in the previous chapter, pairs may need to be reassigned in certain cases if there is to be any possibility of attaining instructional and behavioral objectives.

When the project leader has developed a program that utilizes the efforts of a group of teachers, space in each of their classrooms may be made available. In this situation, a student may be uncomfortable in leaving his or her own classroom to work in another. The problem simply may be unfamiliarity with other school settings. In such an instance, the teacher may want to deal with the feelings being expressed by the student or may wish to accommodate the student's wishes by scheduling the pair in the child's home classroom. An alternative that must be explored carefully before implementation is using the adjustment to a new and unfamiliar environment as a learning experience. Behavioral objectives for the student may center on just this point.

There are many possible spaces in which the tutorial dyads can meet. These include empty rooms in the school building. Few schools have rooms that are unused throughout the day. However, when available, rooms can be modified to meet the needs of your specific project. Some rooms may be available on a parttime basis, and can be scheduled for use ahead of time. Access to rooms on a short-notice basis is not recommended, as will become apparent later (see section on consistency). The library, art room, special education or resource classrooms, the band room, science classrooms, and other special assignment classrooms can be suitable spaces in which to tutor.

A very common place for the tutoring pairs to work is in the classrooms of the participating teachers. Children can meet in several areas in the classroom. One frequently observed location has been the closets placed around the classroom. Children quickly adapt to the small space, and often prefer this very private setting. Other places to meet are in hallways, the cafeteria, and in the auditorium. Hallways can be fine places to work, but there are definite drawbacks. One teacher was very creative in developing cardboard carrels in which tutoring pairs could work in relative quiet. These carrels were placed in a hallway to alleviate space pressures in the classroom. Students were asked to avoid the carrel area when the carrels were in use and to walk very quietly when tutoring was in progress. All was going well until the Fire Marshal visited the school one day to give a talk on fire safety. The school was in violation of the city's fire code by having "obstructions" in the hallway. The carrels were quickly removed.

Some schools have outdoor tables that can be used as a meeting place for the tutorial partners. Some children are able to work even with the distractions afforded by an outdoor setting. In another case, involving a parochial school, the chapel was very close to the school and the children were able to work in the pews. As may be evident from the preceding discussion, tutoring can occur just about anywhere that the students can fit in safely and with comfort. The closeness of the spacing arrangements must be considered in light of the many distractions that can impinge on the young learners' awareness.

Modifications of Settings for Tutoring

Given the space in which to work and the freedom to modify that space, the teacher can make structural changes to improve the comfort of the partners and the likelihood that they will stay on task. Carrels have been discussed as one method of restricting visual distractions for a child. Carrels may be placed in many areas of a classroom and may be positioned so that students cannot see, without turning completely around, other pairs working. Large refrigerator boxes can be positioned to create little areas in which students can work. A rug on the floor can add to the students' comfort. Rugs may be placed in several areas of the room and be identified as tutoring areas. Partitions of a variety of materials and heights can serve to define the tutoring area, as well as to cut down on visual distractions. A very simple solution to the definition of tutoring space is the placement of tape or string around the proposed area. This method has been used successfully for tutoring and other individualized work with children.

As any teacher already knows, many students can work as comfortably seated on the floor as in a chair. These students also may produce the same quality of work in either location. The student who needs the body positioning offered by a chair placed close to a desk or who works better when allowed to spread out can be placed, at the teacher's convenience, in the most appropriate area during the tutoring session.

Students usually can focus more intensively on the task at hand when they are able to establish eye contact with each other. In these instances, face-to-face placement of the partners will be the recommended seating arrangement. Some children are uncomfortable in this seating, or for a variety of reasons work better when seated beside the tutor. For example, the tutor can read the partner's materials a little more easily when seated beside the tutee. As a consequence, the tutor may be able to react more quickly to the tutee's responses. The teacher can determine, before the tutoring project begins, the best seating arrangements for individual partners, or may decide to go with a particular seating arrangement. The authors suggest that the teacher experiment with such arrangements before beginning a program.

The space in which the pairs meet should be relatively free of visual and auditory distractions. Research with problem learners, who comprise the bulk of children being tutored, indicates that attention to the task at hand can be achieved more readily in a low- rather than a high-distraction environment. The visually and auditorily "quiet" environment has been recommended by many teachers for the tutorial learning space. However, the authors have observed learning to occur in peer tutoring projects conducted in some of the noisiest and visually confusing classrooms imaginable. Perhaps more important than the teacher's tolerance and ability to work with distractions is the saliency of those distractions to the children in the classroom. Day-to-day norms of noise and motion in the classroom may be the best indicator of the space requirements for the tutorial program.

The authors recommend that the location of each tutorial session be determined and scheduled for the students in advance of the beginning of the project; we base this recommendation on the need for consistency in the operation of a peer tutoring program, a need which we will discuss at length later in this chapter. The locations will be determined in part by the availability of rooms at the times the students themselves are available, but the teachers should make every effort to have individual pairs meet in the same work spaces throughout the course of the tutorial program.

Time Factors

Tutoring programs vary widely in the length of time they extend into the school year. Number and length of sessions per week likewise vary, depending on certain characteristics of the local situation. One consideration of scheduling is the time of day to conduct the tutorial sessions. Existing daily schedules may determine the times that can be used for the tutorial sessions. We will discuss alternatives to each of those procedures for determining appropriate times for tutoring.

Here is an example of how time factors can influence the success of a project. Mrs. Waters, a third grade teacher, was an enthusiastic believer in the potential of peer tutoring. She had observed her children learning in previous tutorial programs that focused upon reading and spelling. When Mr. Johnson, a fifth grade teacher, told Mrs. Waters that he was working with six children who were capable of working at grade level in arithmetic but were not doing so, she suggested that these children tutor some third graders on math concepts. Noting their class schedules, the two teachers thought that the forty-five-minute period prior to lunch would be the best time for the children to work. After training and orientation, the children were paired and work began. However, the children seemed curiously slow and seemingly uninvolved with the learning task at hand. When Mrs. Waters and Mr. Johnson asked their students for feedback on their behavior, they found that the third graders were restless and hungry, while the fifth graders were tired from the gym period they had just before tutoring. The teachers examined the classroom period schedules again and decided to have the pairs meet during second period in the morning. Following the change in the schedule, the children were observed to be working more enthusiastically and had no difficulty in staying on task.

This example underlines a point with which most teachers are very familiar: children's energy, and consequently their enthusiasm for academic work, typically runs in cycles that reflect the time of day, their health, and the demands on their systems by the home and school environment. Children usually are spilling over with energy at the beginning of the school day. This energy dissipates quickly, especially with the younger child. However, energy quickly returns with rest or food. Of course, there are those children who appear to never tire, but these children will not so much influence scheduling decisions as they will the structuring of the tutorial demands to keep them on task.

A good time for younger children to work is in the first two hours of the school day. There is no firm cutoff age to help in the decision whether students will work better with this time arrangement. The teacher already has knowledge of the capacities of children to stay on task at given points in the day. As students go to middle schools and high schools, they are conditioned to assume more and more demands on their powers of concentration. The task of scheduling older students for a tutorial program thus becomes easier in that it is possible to schedule tutoring sessions over the entire school day. The teacher should keep in mind that even older students have energy highs and lows during the day. Before lunch and after gym are the periods during which few students can maintain full motivation toward academic assignments.

Other factors over which there is little or no control can affect the ability of a child to work at maximum efficiency in a tutorial arrangement. For example, the child who is ill, whether on a long or short-term basis, and who persists in coming to school, seldom is able either to concentrate fully or to work effectively with other children. Obviously, it usually is preferable not to have children tutor when they are sick, because of the risks of infection. Many children come to school with an inadequate or no breakfast. As a result, they may be listless and unwilling to work during the morning. One school which had operated a small tutorial project for two years noticed that more was accomplished during morning sessions when a breakfast program was introduced at their school during the third year of the project's operation. Overall, there is little control over this factor, which can affect tutoring programs. Contacts with parents through the school nurse, social worker, or other means can stress the impact of nutritional factors on the child's ability to perform in the classroom.

The teacher may decide to schedule the students in accordance with the energy levels of the children, in accordance with the pre-existing availability of free time periods, or with some combination of the two. Whatever the arrangement, the need for consistency of the scheduling remains important. An effort should be made to have children meet at the same time period each day of tutoring. This is important for several reasons. Students quickly learn a schedule which does not vary on a daily basis. They can get to work without having to go through a brief period of reorientation at the beginning of each session. They will be at approximately the same level of energy and motivation throughout the project. This consideration will have more importance in those programs which have a strong research orientation.

Length of Sessions

An important decision for the teacher to make concerns the length of each tutorial session. There are several alternatives available, all of which have been used in other projects. To illustrate, it may be possible to turn the children loose to work as long as they want. The teacher may schedule tutorial pairs to meet throughout the length of specific periods in the day. In addition, it may be necessary to limit the length of a session, according to the goals and objectives of the program. Before considering these alternatives, the research of Ellson and his colleagues (1968) can give some perspective on the limits of a child's ability to remain on task. In this particular programmed tutoring activity with children in kindergarten and the first grade, a total of fifteen minutes devoted to tutoring was the maximum length of time that these student could concentrate on materials. Presumably, as the students become older, they can stay on task longer.

As noted previously, the goals and objectives of the program affect the decisions made at each point in the program. When the teacher has limited objectives for the children or believes that they should be given control over the decision of length of sessions, then the decision about length of sessions can be left open or allowed to vary during the progress of the program. If a pilot study has been included as part of the overall evaluation design, it will be possible to assess the impact of session length on tutorial outcomes. An additional consideration is that allowing the students to determine the length of a session may be one of the more valuable learning experiences of the tutorial program. Children can readily assume this responsibility, as the authors have found from their observation of several programs. The children may make more demands on themselves than the teacher would ever consider making.

Another alternative that has been mentioned regarding the scheduling of session length was the duration of specific tutorial periods. The decision as to how long a given tutorial period should be would include consideration of the ability and tolerance level of the tutor and tutee and the capacity to complete an assignment, according to prespecified procedures, at the desired level of performance. The length of time the tutor and tutee are able to stay on task can affect this decision. Equally important in making the decision is consideration of the countless bits of information that have been accumulated regarding the cognitive and behavioral abilities of participating students.

The research-based tutorial project described at length earlier in this chapter is one example of a program in which the objectives of the program influenced the length of sessions. In this example, there was a daily tutoring goal that entailed the tutee's learning ten spelling words. The project director attempted to structure the sessions so that students worked at the tutoring task for approximately the same length of time during the entire project. Other tutoring programs similarly control the length of sessions to meet research demands for consistency of arrangements across pairs, and for related reasons. The length of sessions may be monitored so that several different time arrangements across sessions may be emphasized by the teacher to the tutors. This emphasis can become part of the pre-tutorial training program, and be reinforced periodically throughout the length of the project.

Number of Sessions

The teacher's next concern in structuring a tutorial program is the number of sessions to schedule for each pair. A superficial answer (that needs much explanation) is "as many sessions as are needed." What determines the need is unique with the specific tutoring program. At the point that it is decided to go through the process of developing a tutorial program, an estimation will already have been made regarding the needs of the students to be met by tutoring. These needs may have been interpreted in the form of objectives as being academic, social, or some combination of the two. Dependent upon the stated objectives, the amount of work necessary to develop materials and schedule sessions will vary considerably. In some instances, it may not be possible to attain all objectives in the course of the academic year. Even given the assistance of an instructional aide, the task may be too great, but the teacher should not be discouraged. Important allies are students, who can help to develop materials, monitor session quality and length, and assist in the administration of all forms and evaluation measures. If the scope of the program is small, whether in number of children or in the extent of the objectives for the students, a program to meet the individual needs of children is well within reach.

Many teachers who have worked on peer tutoring projects have decided to schedule the number of sessions to reflect an estimated average ability of the students to meet the instructional and behavioral objectives. The teacher also may restrict the number of sessions to meet other limitations. For example, a physical space for tutoring may not, for some reason, be available after the mid-semester break. Consequently, sessions may have to be terminated at that point until another area can be reserved. Teachers may limit the number of sessions per tutorial pair so that other children either can receive tutoring or get to tutor. This should not, however, be a common occurrence. Every child who has the desire or the need for tutoring should have access to these services, provided there are sufficient materials and space to allot for the tutoring.

Deterline (1970) has provided some cues that may be helpful when scheduling times for the tutorial pairs. It is his suggestion that tutorial sessions should not be scheduled during time periods that also contain activities that are highly preferred by the children. Students can become upset or feel penalized if they are made to miss a really interesting activity because of scheduling for tutoring. Another suggestion is that tutoring pairs not be assigned to rooms in which other students are studying. The tutoring activities will very probably bother the other students, who may in turn distract the students in the tutorial dyad. If there are a number of distractions that persist throughout the duration of the tutorial project, the teacher can expect the participating students to go through an adjustment period to compensate for the surrounding distractions.

MONITORING THE TUTORING PROGRAM

One common finding reported by teachers is that the regularity and consistency of meetings by the tutorial pair over the term of the project is more important than the length or number of tutoring sessions. A good rule of thumb is that once a schedule is established, stick to it. Early in the tutor training component of a tutorial program, the tutors must be impressed with the importance of being prepared to meet on time and in a specific location for each session. Emphasize the importance of being a *reliable* tutor. The tutor, in his or her function as a model for the tutee, is demonstrating something that the tutee would do well to imitate. The consistency of arrangements is reassuring to the child being tutored. The child who is familiar with the tutoring arrangements can then devote all energies to learning the tutorial materials.

In the last chapter, the authors discussed Harrison's suggestions for training tutors. To restate them:

1   Put the child being tutored at ease.
2   Clarify the tutorial task.
3   Show the child being tutored how to verify an answer, when this is part of the program's structure.
4   Have the partner read each problem aloud.
5   Provide feedback to the partner only after that person has made an overt response.
6   Have the partner verify each response.
7   Avoid punishment.
8   Provide appropriate verbal praise.
9   Provide a reward when this conforms to program objectives.
10 Evaluate mastery on designated items.

Harrison's training program is an example of the attention that can be given to details of the tutorial process. Once such details have been specified in the program, the basis by which it is possible to monitor and, eventually, to evaluate the tutorial program has been created. The progress of each tutor in complying with the established specifications for procedure and for interaction with students can be effectively monitored, in addition to the progress by the child being tutored. The importance of maintaining the performance criteria presented to the tutors in their training sessions is evident when considering Harrison's finding that untrained tutors did not accomplish much in terms of meeting learning objectives—the trained tutors had partners who learned significantly more than did the partners of untrained tutors.

The teacher who has developed a tutor training program probably will have built into that program criteria for skill attainment. Student tutors should not be allowed to work with other students until they can show the project director that they have acquired the prerequisite skills contained in the training component. Tutors should be encouraged to come to the project director with questions and concerns throughout the duration of the tutoring program. While tutors must feel free to do this, the teacher is responsible for, and in control of, the progression and implementation of the program. The teacher's major concerns are as follows:

1   Are the tutors introducing materials as scheduled and following all prespecified procedures?
2   Are the program's goals being met?

To answer these questions, the teacher can monitor several processes that should be occurring. The orientation of tutor to partner is observable. Pairs can be checked to see that they are meeting in assigned spaces, at assigned times, and for the assigned number of sessions. The seating arrangements, if prespecified, can similarly be observed. The instructional demands of the program on the tutor and the partner can be assessed next. The monitor can determine whether the tutor is presenting the correct materials in the right sequence and with the appropriate level of feedback to the partner. For example, if verbal praise is being used, the monitor can assess the tutor's performance in giving trained responses at an appropriate frequency. The child being tutored also is monitored on meeting the structured instructional demands. The tutee should be working, focusing attention on the learning task. The tutee should be giving responses that indicate both involvement in the learning task and a degree of success in that task. When the child being tutored appears to the monitor to be uninvolved or not learning, the teacher can discuss with the tutor ways either to make the task more interesting or to make instructional goals more realistic for that student.

The next important component of the monitoring process is the relationship of the tutor with the partner. The students, and especially the tutor who, presumably, has been trained in this, should be working with a minimum of friction. The partners should have much eye contact, should both be focused on task, and should be able to work together in a friendly and cooperative manner. We have discussed previously the possibility of reassigning pairs who do not work well together. Careful monitoring of tutorial dyads can reveal very early in the program problems in the relationship of the partners so that it will be possible to intervene when problem behaviors are first evidenced.

While teachers vary in the amount of supervision they feel is necessary with individual tutorial pairs, a wise rule is to observe one in every three sessions to check on the functioning of the tutoring pair. This rule of thumb has resulted from the authors' experiences with a variety of tutorial programs. The amount of supervision usually becomes more extensive in programs that have an involved or very specific research design. In such cases, individual sessions can require daily supervision.

The project director can recruit other teachers or aides to help with the monitoring process. It should now be obvious that such helpers will need to be trained in elements of the program's design to insure that the monitoring is both accurate and inclusive. Occasionally, students can be involved in such activities. One way to avoid much of the burden of monitoring each pair to insure that they correctly implement the tutorial program is to stagger the starting times of the tutoring pairs. For example, in a program which will have twenty tutorial pairs involved, the project director can have five pairs begin each week over a period of four weeks. Monitoring of the pairs starting for the first time in a given week can be very extensive, with less supervision applied to the other pairs that have been more extensively involved.

Simplification of the monitoring process can be accomplished by employing a monitoring evaluation form that may be developed from the instructional and behavioral objectives of the tutor and the child being tutored. A checklist can be created that, first, can be employed to assess the utilization of each of the elements and, second, can be used with a simple measure rating the effectiveness of the utilization of that component. Figure 4.1 represents a sample checklist appropriate for this purpose. A checklist on the instructional and behavioral elements that have been incorporated into the design of the tutorial program then can be used by monitors as they assess implementation of the tutorial components. Figures 4.2 and 4.3 are sample monitoring checklists that may be used to assess tutor and learner behaviors during a tutorial session. Whatever checklist that has been created for the project can have attached to it an evaluation measure that can yield additional data for research purposes. The checklist with rating scale can give teachers "hard data" that can be used in decisions to retrain tutors, to change instructional strategies or

FIGURE 4.1.   Tutorial Monitoring Form—Sample One

	Tutor Effectiveness (check one per item)		
	Adequate	Needs Some Improvement	Needs Extensive Improvement
Puts child at ease			
Clarifies tutorial task			
Helps tutee verify answer			
Tutee reads answer aloud			
Tutor provides feedback to overt responses only			
Tutee verifies each response			
Tutor avoids punishment			
Tutor provides appropriate verbal praise			
Tutor provides appropriate rewards			
Tutor evaluates mastery on designated items			

FIGURE 4.2. Tutorial Monitoring Form—Sample Two

Tutorial Behaviors Assessment—Check Appropriate Category

	Target Behaviors	*Needs Limited Retraining*	*Needs Extensive Retraining*
Content techniques			
a. Presents materials in appropriate sequence			
b. Presents materials in appropriate manner			
c. Presents materials at scheduled times			
Reinforcement techniques			
a. Provides verbal praise as scheduled			
b. Avoids punishment— verbal and nonverbal			
Tutor/tutee Orientation			
a. Tutor/tutee maintain eye contact			
b. Tutor/tutee seated in programmed manner			

materials, to reassign partners, and to determine a reasonable point to terminate the tutoring program.

As a final note, the monitoring process will provide an abundance of information on the performance of tutors and their partners. Tutors may be uncomfortable in their "teacher" role or unsure of just how well they are doing. The tutor will almost certainly enjoy hearing of the progress that is being made towards the partners' learning goals. A word of encouragement and a positive reflection of the tutor's performance of duties will encourage that child to continue to work hard as a tutor and to use the techniques for which you have reinforced him or her. Let the tutor know that his or her contributions are appreciated.

FIGURE 4.3. Tutorial Monitoring Form—Sample Three

	Percent of Time Behaviors Occur as Specified				
	100%	75%	50%	25%	0%

Temporal Factors
a. Tutor/tutee meet on time
b. Tutor tutee meet for entire scheduled period
c. Tutor controls session tempo appropriately

Space Factors
a. Tutor/tutee meet in scheduled space
b. Tutor makes optimal use of space
c. Tutor maintains quiet during tutorial session

Research/Evaluation Factors
a. Tutor keeps and turns in log as scheduled
b. Tutor completes and turns in all answer sheets
c. Tutor/tutee complete research forms as scheduled

THE EVALUATION COMPONENT

Elements of the evaluation component have been discussed earlier in this chapter. In this section we will focus on the importance of the evaluation process and the effect of evaluation and research decisions on the structure of a tutorial program.

Evaluation of a tutoring program helps the teacher to assess progress towards the predetermined goals and objectives of the program. At the very beginning of the program, a decision is made to recruit students for the tutor and tutee positions. If some measure is used to aid in the selection decision, the value of that measure will be reflected in the success of those students chosen for the tutor or tutee roles. Given any measure of the children's ability, whether these measures are teacher-made or commercially available, the teacher can make a decision on the cutoff scores that will qualify a child for tutorial assignment. (Clearly, this is not an issue when tests are not used, or every child, regardless of score, participates in the tutorial program.) The teacher may have decided to assign students who score 80 percent correct on a diagnostic test to the tutor role positions, and students who score under 50 percent correct to the tutee slots in the program. Once the program is underway and the partners are meeting on schedule, the teacher may discover that some of the tutors have less knowledge of the lesson content than do the children being tutored. Herein lies the importance of a good evaluation component and, in many instances, the utility of a pilot project. The pilot project or study, as discussed earlier, can be used to try out materials, instructional arrangements, and tutorial techniques before teachers begin a large-scale program. The evaluation of students does not always weed out children who are not well qualified to be tutors. However, an evaluation component built into the tutor training program can be sensitive to the tutor's capacities to fulfill the demands of the tutor role. Harrison's tutor training objectives have been discussed as one method of specifying tutor behaviors and skills. This method can be given an evaluation element to assess the perceived performance and attainment of objectives by the tutors during training. The teacher can establish levels of rated competency that must be attained before the child can be assigned to tutor another child. Levels of competency can be defined, either from the accumulation of experiences with children who have been released to work with other students, or through the systematic assessment of the effects of varying levels of rated competency on the tutor's performance and the attainment of learning and behavioral goals by that tutor's partner. A pilot project can be utilized to investigate this research question.

The evaluation component coincides with elements of the monitoring procedures that we have discussed. To restate, the evaluation of the data that result from monitoring the tutor and tutee helps the project staff make decisions about progress in the tutoring sessions and the attainment of tutorial objectives. With this information, the teacher can determine which interventions, if any, will be necessary to set the partners back on course towards the learning goals. The information is helpful to the teacher in determining whether the goals and objectives need to be modified to fit the reality of the performance of the children. The tutor training program can be changed to focus on additional instructional or communication skills to help the tutor meet session objectives. Feedback from the evaluation process also can suggest new directions for future tutorial programs.

Feedback to the tutor on his or her use of tutoring strategies typically follows the evaluation of their monitored performance. Some teachers have found a way to communicate information on the tutor's performance that is nonthreatening, as well as an incentive to work on changing behaviors. These teachers have used variations of the tutor feedback charts (see Figures 4.1 through 4.5). On these charts, which can be introduced during the tutor training sessions, the program director outlines the specific expectations of tutor performance and the means by which this performance will be assessed. The tutors are told that their performance will be monitored at regular intervals during the course of the project, and that information on their use of tutorial strategies will be collected. This information, rated in some fashion (whether in terms of frequency of occurrence, or simply the use or nonuse of specific techniques), is then given to the tutor in chart form. While the chart is not absolutely necessary, it does allow the tutor to quickly grasp progress toward the attainment of objectives. The tutors can be trained to monitor their own performance. As part of the journal or log that they are keeping on daily sessions, the tutors can rate themselves on use of instructional and communication techniques and the frequency of such usage.

Evaluation of the tutorial program's effectiveness can be assessed in terms of process objectives and/or product objectives. Under the first category will likely be such process factors as the "climate" of the tutorial sessions. Process factors rarely have been investigated in peer tutoring programs. Product factors are represented by the performance of tutees on learning posttests, reflecting the attainment of instructional objectives. Evaluation of process and product factors can be described more appropriately as part of the research design of

---

FIGURE 4.4. Teacher Observation Form

Tutor _____   *Date of Observation* _____

Tutee _____

		Yes	No	Not Observed
1	The tutor was prepared for the lesson.			
2	The tutor had the necessary materials available.			
3	The tutor demonstrated acceptable knowledge of basic concepts being taught.			
4	The tutor gave clear directions.			
5	The tutor used positive reinforcement.			
6	The tutor used negative reinforcement.			
7	The tutor used frequent reinforcement.			
8	The tutor maintained eye contact with the tutee.			
9	The tutor actively involved the tutee in the lesson.			
10	The tutor was enthusiastic.			
11	The tutor kept the tutee on task.			
12	The tutee appeared interested during the session.			
13	The tutee attempted to perform lesson tasks.			
14	The tutee completed lesson assignments.			

Adapted from: Laffey, J., and Perkins, P. *Teacher orientation handbook.* Washington, D.C.: National Reading Center Foundation. (ERIC Document Reproduction No. 068-460)

the tutorial program. Many programs do not contain a research component for assessing scientifically the outcomes of the tutorial sessions. A common alternative to a research design is reliance on anecdotal accounts of the success of the program. Teachers speak of the changes in children who have participated in the tutorial

FIGURE 4.5. Teacher Observation Form

Tutor _____   *Date of Observation* _____

Tutee _____

Lesson Preparation

1   Had the tutor prepared material for the session? _____
2   Did the tutor have the necessary material for the lesson available?

Lesson Presentation

1   What was the objective of the lesson? _____
2   What activities did the tutor use? _____
3   What materials were used by the tutor? _____
4   Did the materials relate to the tutee's classroom lessons? _____
5   How did the tutor handle the materials? _____
6   What type of directions were given by the tutor? _____
7   Did the tutor actively involve the tutee in the lesson? If so, how?

8   What type of reinforcement was used by the tutor? _____
9   How frequently did the tutor reinforce the tutee during the session?

10   What type of work skills were exhibited by the tutee? _____

11   How did the tutee respond to the session? _____
12   What kind of relationship did the tutor and tutee appear to have?

Adapted from: Laffey, J., and Perkins, P. *Teacher orientation handbook.* Washington, D.C.: National Reading Center Foundation. (ERIC Document Reproduction No. 068-460) project. There is, however, no assurance that the changes have occurred in the children's performance rather than in the teacher's *perceptions* of the children's performance. If, at the close of a tutoring program, it is necessary to document that a given project was successful, an evaluation component to the program will provide the data to make a realistic statement. A sample tutor evaluation form (Figure 4.6) can provide objective feedback on tutor performance.

The evaluation design need not be extensive. For example, it may be adequate simply to determine if learning has occurred on the part of the tutors or tutees. Giving a pretest and a posttest on the tutorial content will provide some indication that learning has or has not occurred. If the evaluation objectives are more extensive and attempt to reflect principles of experimental design (such as the use of control groups), then scheduling needs for *research* purposes should reflect at all times the translation of various research hypotheses into an appropriate time frame for assessment of process and product variables. Forms for research purposes are easily constructed to test research hypotheses. In some instances, measures and rating scales will be available in the literature, easily adapted for most research designs. When not available, the project director will be required to develop and, whenever possible, test for usefulness (reliability and validity) evaluation measures for the project's specific objectives. A test to assess pretutorial and post-tutorial knowledge of math concepts is an example of one teacher-made measure. A more elaborate example of the development and use of process and product measures has been discussed several times in this book. Earlier in this chapter, we outlined the structure of a tutorial program in spelling. The program incorporated a peer-mediated instruction approach. Several process and product measures were created to test particular hypotheses about the operation of these factors. The measure which assessed learning of spelling words was a 200-word posttest that contained words drawn from a 500-word pretest. A 100-word spelling list was used to measure generalization of learning.

Several tutor and tutee characteristics were measured and analyzed for their effects on process and product factors. Characteristics that were measured included peer status and liking for the tutorial partner. The peer status measure used as a pretest was a variation of the Revised Ohio Social Acceptance Scale, Advanced Series (Forlan and Wrightstone, 1955). Each child in the class received a peer acceptance

---

FIGURE 4.6. Sample Tutor Evaluation Form

Tutor _____   *Session Dates* _____

Number of Sessions _____

Rank the tutor in the following areas from 1 through 4.

1	The tutor was regular in attendance.	1	2	3	4
2	The tutor was on time for sessions.	1	2	3	4
3	The tutor established a good relationship with the tutee.	1	2	3	4
4	The tutor was enthusiastic.	1	2	3	4
5	The tutor used positive reinforcement.	1	2	3	4
6	The tutor used negative reinforcement.	1	2	3	4
7	The tutor demonstrated model behaviors.	1	2	3	4
8	The tutor exhibited proper speech.	1	2	3	4
9	The tutor cooperated with the tutee's teacher.	1	2	3	4
10	The tutor followed the teacher's directions.	1	2	3	4
11	The tutor maintained good daily records.	1	2	3	4
12	The tutor demonstrated initiative in planning for the sessions.	1	2	3	4
13	The tutor displayed adequate knowledge of subject matter.	1	2	3	4
14	The tutor gave clear directions.	1	2	3	4
15	The tutor asked effective questions.	1	2	3	4
16	The tutor involved the tutee in the lesson.	1	2	3	4
17	The tutor maintained the tutee's attention during the session.	1	2	3	4
18	The tutor seemed to enjoy the sessions.	1	2	3	4

Adapted from: Laffey, J., and Perkins, P. *Teacher orientation handbook.* Washington, D.C.: National Reading Center Foundation. (ERIC Document Reproduction No. 068-460)

and peer rejection score based on group responses. The liking scales for the partners were similar for tutor and tutee. The tutor was given a list of five names. The names included that of the child to be tutored and of classmates randomly included on the list. The tutor rank-ordered the five in terms of whom he liked the most of the five, whom he liked second best, and so on. The tutee received a list of five names, including that of the tutor, to rank-order in a similar manner.

This study also investigated the effects of process factors on the product factors. The process measures were scales of perceived affect and perceived competency of the tutorial partner. These scales (found in Addendum 4B of this chapter) represented modifications of scales from other sources. Items for the perceived competency were suggested by findings from a task force on teacher competency and coincided with the style of items on an experimental measure of perceived affect and competency. The perceived affect scales (A)-TR and (A)-TE, and the perceived competency scales, (C)-TR and (C)-TE, represent the researcher's efforts to combine the best of existing instruments and experimental findings with his desire to test hypotheses.

As an additional element of the research design, a digit-span score of short-term memory was obtained on tutored students by giving them a subtest of a standardized test of intelligence. This test was given to guarantee an important element of experimental design, control. The researcher's objective was to determine if the mastery of the spelling lists was the result of the tutorial techniques, or the operation of superior memory skills by any subject of the experimental group. Similar uses of measures to ensure the soundness of a research design may be necessary under the special circumstances of a program's research component.

The reader may have other questions on the structuring of a tutorial program to meet the needs of the tutor, the needs of the child being tutored, and the needs of the project director who is attempting to demonstrate the effectiveness of the program. By keeping the philosophy of the program as the guiding force and following our approach to break down the tutorial process into small elements and then evaluating the effectiveness of these elements, the reader can create solutions to problems of structure in program implementation. The teacher has a resource in dealing with the intricacies of structuring a tutoring program in those colleagues who have worked with this or similar types of individualized instruction. Both the successes and failures of these professionals have been helpful to us in developing our programs. The children who have experienced the tutorial approach are not only an inspiration and an incentive to continue such programs, but are often the ones who have the most to suggest by way of changes in tutorial procedures and structuring of elements. Such children in your school can be involved in providing feedback from the very beginning of the tutorial program.

Addendum 4A
SAMPLE FORMS
FROM A PEER TUTORIAL PROGRAM

TUTOR LOG FOR WEEK BEGINNING _____

Your name:
Your student's name:

Day of Week	Time Met	Regular or Makeup (If makeup, give the reason for missing regular session)	Comments on the Student
Monday			
Tuesday			
Wednesday			
Thursday			
Friday			

Additional Comments:

LESSON SHEET NUMBER _____

Your name: Date:
Student's name: Note: Trial word underlined

Word Number	Word	Sample Sentence	Repeat Word	Times Tried by the Student
One				
Two				
Three				
Four				
Five				
Six				
Seven				
Eight				
Nine				
Ten				

ANSWER SHEET

Your name: Date:
Tutor's name: Time completed (see aide):

Word Number				Trial			
	1	2	3	4	5	6	7
One							
Two							
Three							
Four							
Five							
Six							
Seven							
Eight							
Nine							
Ten							

Addendum 4B
SAMPLE RESEARCH INSTRUMENTS
FROM A PEER
TUTORIAL PROJECT

"THESE ARE MY FRIENDS" SCALE

We don't like all of our friends in the same way. Some we like more than others. There may be some people we don't like at all.

The checklist below contains five different descriptions of your friends in this classroom. Below the descriptions are the names of the other boys and girls in the class. Across from each name down the page, put a check in the space under the statement which most nearly describes your feeling about the person. Do not place a check beside your name, but place a check beside the name of every other student in this class.

No one in your room will see this paper.

Name of Classmate	Very, very best friends	Good friends	Not friends but is okay	I don't know this person	We are not friends and he (she) is not okay to me

LIKING SCALE

Everyone likes some people more than others. On the form below are five names of your classmates. Your task is to rank the five students as follows: Place a 1 beside the name of the person you like the most of the five. Put a 2 beside the name of the one you like the next best. Put a 3 beside the one you like the next best, and so on for 4 and 5.

Rank *all* of the students. You need not sign your name.

TUTORING SESSION RATING SCALE (C)-TE

Name: _____   Date: _____

Directions: During your experiences as a tutor, you and your partner worked closely on learning how to spell words. You probably can remember a lot about what happened during your tutoring sessions. Below are nine statements that may describe your working relationship with your tutoring partner.

For each of the statements, check off the phrase that most nearly reflects the truth of that statement for you, as you remember your partner during the tutoring sessions. Remember that this rating scale is intended to describe only the times that you and your partner were tutoring together.

Sample item:	The student pronounced words softly.	Always true	True most of the time	True about half of the time	Seldom true	Never true

If you remember that your partner never pronounced words softly during a tutoring session, you would place a check under the "Never true" column.

Item	*Always true*	*True most of the time*	*True about half of the time*	*Seldom true*	*Never true*
1 I never had the feeling that the student knew what he(she) was doing.					
2 The student took responsibility for learning the materials in a lesson.					
3 It seemed to me that the student didn't take his(her) work seriously.					
4 The student gave his (her) answers clearly and carefully.					
5 I would like to work with my partner again.					
6 I thought my student did a good job.					
7 The student seemed to be in pretty good control of himself(herself) at all times.					
8 The student had a positive attitude toward learning during our sessions.					
9 The student did everything possible to help us finish on time.					

TUTORING SESSION RATING SCALE (A)-TE

Name: _____ Date: _____

Directions: During your experiences as a tutor, you and your partner worked closely together on learning how to spell words. You probably can remember a lot about your perceptions of your partner during the tutoring sessions. Below are nine statements that may describe your perceptions of your tutoring partner.

For each of the statements, check off the phrase that most nearly reflects the truth of that statement for you, as you remember your partner during the tutoring sessions. Remember that this rating scale is intended to describe only the times that you and your partner were tutoring together.

| *Sample item*: | The student made me feel helpful. | Always true | True most of the time | True about half of the time | Seldom true | Never true |

If you remember that your partner made you feel helpful during most of the sessions, you would place a check under the "True most of the time" column.

Item	Always true	True most of the time	True about half of the time	Seldom true	Never true
1 The student was a likeable person.					
2 I had the feeling that here was a person that I could really trust.					
3 It was easy to talk to the student. He(she) seemed interested.					
4 I always had the feeling that I was only another student as far as my partner was concerned.					
5 The student expressed feelings openly with me.					
6 The student treated me with respect.					
7 The student did not make fun of me.					
8 The student made comments to me that made me feel good.					
9 The student listened carefully to what I had to say.					

TUTORING SESSION RATING SCALE (A)-TR

Name: _____   Date: _____

Directions: During your experiences of being tutored, you and your partner worked closely on learning how to spell words. You probably can remember a lot about your perceptions of your partner during the tutoring sessions. Below are nine statements that may describe the perceptions of your tutoring partner.

  For each of the statements, check off the phrase that most nearly reflects the truth of that statement for you, as you remember your partner during the tutoring sessions. Remember that this rating scale is intended to describe only the times that you and your partner were tutoring together.

| *Sample item*: | The tutor made me feel helpful. | Always true | True most of the time | True about half of the time | Seldom true | Never true |

If you remember that your partner made you feel helpful during most of the sessions, you would place a check under the "True most of the time" column for that item.

Item	*Always true*	*True most of the time*	*True about half of the time*	*Seldom true*	*Never true*
1 The tutor was a likeable person.					
2 I had the feeling that here was a person that I could really trust.					
3 It was easy to talk to the tutor. He(she) seemed interested.					
4 I always had the feeling that I was only another student as far as my partner was concerned.					
5 The tutor expressed feelings openly with me.					
6 The tutor treated me with respect.					
7 The tutor did not make fun of me.					
8 The tutor made comments to me that made me feel good.					
9 The tutor listened carefully to what I had to say.					

TUTORING SESSION RATING SCALE (C)-TR

Name: _____ Date: _____

Directions: During your experiences of being tutored, you and your partner worked closely on learning how to spell words. You probably can remember a lot about what happened during your tutoring sessions. Below are nine statements that may describe your working relationship with your tutoring partner.

For each of the statements, check off the phrase that most nearly reflects the truth of that statement for you, as you remember your partner during the tutoring sessions. Remember that this rating scale is intended to describe only the times that you and your partner were tutoring together.

Sample item: The tutor pronounced words softly.	Always true	True most of the time	True about half of the time	Seldom true	Never true

If you remember that your tutor never pronounced words softly during a tutoring session, you would place a check under the "Never true" column.

Item	*Always true*	*True most of the time*	*True about half of the time*	*Seldom true*	*Never true*
1 I never had the feeling that the tutor knew what he(she) was doing.					
2 The tutor took responsibility for teaching the materials in a lesson.					
3 It seemed to me that the tutor didn't take his (her) work very seriously.					
4 The tutor presented the words clearly and carefully.					
5 I would like to work with my partner again.					
6 I thought my tutor did a good job.					
7 The tutor seemed to be in pretty good control of himself (herself) at all times.					
8 The tutor had a positive attitude toward learning during the sessions.					
9 The tutor did everything possible to help me finish on time.					

5

DEVELOPING THE CONTENT OF A PEER TUTORING PROGRAM

Previous chapters have suggested structural considerations in establishing a peer tutoring program. Incorporated within these chapters have been guidelines for the creation of tutoring programs, the delineation of goals and objectives, and discussion of how to create a setting in which a tutorial program can best be conducted. In this chapter, we will discuss elements which need to be considered when determining the content of a program, and procedures for matching materials to activities so that stated program goals may be best achieved.

Creating objectives for each child in a tutoring program is a formidable task, especially when the teacher is attempting to initiate changes in the tutor as well as the child being tutored. While the use of tutorial materials will flow naturally from the objectives specified for a particular program, in general the more clearly stated and definite the objectives, the easier it will be to locate the appropriate materials with which to work on that objective. Before proceeding with considerations on the content of tutorial programs, let us delve further into the specification of objectives.

There are two broad areas to consider in the creation of objectives for students, i.e., the academic and the social-emotional. In Chapter 4, we discussed setting goals for the tutor and the child being tutored. We are emphasizing here the need for the definition of objectives, whether academic or social-emotional, in carefully articulated behavioral terms. For example, one teacher stated as a goal that a student, Robert, should complete the materials in a grade level reader by the end of the tutorial project. An objective derived from this rather broad goal was that Robert would be able to read the basal text with 80 percent comprehension as indicated by a series of tests covering the entire book. Because Robert's teacher had established already which book would be used to teach reading comprehension, the teacher did not have any difficulty deciding on an appropriate text for the tutorial sessions. The decisions that remained for the teacher to make involved how to present appropriate content within any one session.

As another example, Jennie-Ann's teacher had as a goal that Jennie-Ann would talk more frequently with peers. The teacher's objective was specific to structured situations—Jennie-Ann would initiate the conversation at the beginning of 90 percent of the tutorial sessions. The teacher, during the training phase of the program, talked with the tutors about the importance of starting each session on a friendly note. During the role-playing segment of the training, the teacher made sure that Jennie-Ann practiced the active initiating of conversation with the partner. Jennie-Ann's teacher also structured the administration of materials in such a way that the child was required to be verbal and assertive in presenting lessons. With Jennie-Ann, the coaching worked with a surprising degree of success. She was observed to initiate conversations during every session and to be verbally assertive during the teacher phase of a lesson. Additionally, she carried this new assertiveness back to the classroom, where it survived the termination of the tutorial project.

In this second example, the specification of the social-emotional objective was for the tutor, and actually dealt with only a small segment of the tutoring sessions. The teacher's hope was that training in verbal assertiveness that focused on a small portion of the tutorial session would generalize to other portions of the session and to the broader arena of the classroom. In general, affective goals can be specified for the tutor and the child being tutored, but the translation of these goals into specific objectives is somewhat more difficult. Later in this chapter, we will discuss affective materials as content for tutorial programs so that it will be possible to delineate the social-emotional objectives which could be realized with the use of such materials.

DESIGNING A PEER TUTORING PROGRAM

As with any educational endeavor, there are a number of steps that must be considered prior to the successful initiation of a long term activity. Establishing a peer tutoring program is no exception. Deterline (1970) states that at the most basic level, all teachers who will be participating in the tutorial project must be identified. Once teachers have been acquainted with the idea of a peer tutoring program, it is possible to recruit both the thoughts and efforts of other teachers to make the tutoring program a reality. Of course, if the tutoring project is intended to be a cross-age program, at least two teachers will have to cooperate in the scheduling of children for tutoring. In all probability, several teachers will express an interest in joining a tutorial program. It may become the responsibility of the teacher who initiates the project to coordinate arrangements in establishing the program. In programs where several teachers are involved, it is important that one individual be appointed to serve as the project director (i.e., the person who will schedule both the placement and meeting times of the partners). In an earlier chapter, we discussed the impact of evaluation on the total tutorial program. In certain instances, outside researchers may assume the responsibility for designating length of sessions, procedures to be followed, and materials used. It is still recommended that an on-site person, whether teacher or administrator, be responsible for monitoring the daily operations of the program.

Once the teachers who will be participating in the program have been identified, it is necessary to specify the materials that will comprise the content of the tutoring sessions (later in this chapter the development of materials will be discussed). The content of the materials will serve as practice materials during the training of tutors, and may be incorporated further into the evaluation instruments that are part of the research design. The quantity of materials available to form the content of a program determines, to a large degree, the amount of work that will be necessary in creating additional materials or in modifying existing materials to meet the specific needs of the program. The project director will be responsible for determining content needs of the individual students, as well as determining (1) the materials to use in the training sessions, (2) the materials used to introduce learning concepts, (3) the materials necessary to supplement introductory materials, and (4) the materials appropriate for the review of earlier presented concepts.

Program directors differ in the importance they place on planning for session content. In some programs it is possible to specify at the beginning of the project the content of each session's lesson. Indeed, this is possible because the content of sessions is dictated by the goals of the project. For example, when the goal of a tutoring program is to master a 2000-word spelling list in 50 sessions, then 40 words should represent an optimal learning load for each session. Other program directors plan lessons on a day-to-day or a week-to-week basis and find that this arrangement is quite satisfactory to meet the goals of the program; but these individuals must be remarkably anxiety-free to proceed on such a short-term basis. Lesson planning tends to become more diverse as the program progresses, and the individual needs of children require variations in lesson design.

Planning for affective-oriented materials frequently is more difficult, especially if the goals of the program are entirely affective in nature. Usually, however, the affective goals are of secondary importance to the academic goals. While there are a few packets of affective materials that can be modified to meet the needs of a tutorial program, such materials will usually have to be devised and constructed on-site. When the affective goals are specified so that they can be achieved through the modeling of responses or through the tutorial processes rather than the content, such goals can be readily realized.

One illustration of this is provided from the authors' experiences in a school that had adopted the peer tutorial approach to meet many of the academic and affective needs of its children. Miss Williamson was concerned when Ben would not concentrate on his assignments and expressed feelings of failure in math class. She was able to secure a tutor and establish an ongoing tutorial program. The tutor, Bill, was three years older than Ben, and was himself uncertain about his academic abilities in math. Miss Williamson provided all the materials for Bill, and stressed with him the importance of mastering all the math problems to be presented. Since the materials were four grade levels below his own grade placement, Bill was able to accomplish this quickly. He approached his first session with Ben with confidence. Following a specific procedure for problem-solving, he was able to present math concepts clearly and help Ben to solve all the problems. Having been coached to give an abundance of rewarding remarks to the tutee, Bill was the model of a successful and confident student. Ben achieved grade level after sixteen weeks of tutoring from Bill. Bill carried his new-found confidence in math back to his classroom, where he also gained approximately one grade level by the completion of the tutoring program.

Once the tutor has met with the tutee and is working on the chosen materials, the project director, in many instances, will have to insure that *tutors are always cognizant of the correct responses*. In one tutorial program (Ehly, 1975) focusing upon the subject area of spelling, tutors were provided a Lesson Sheet on which each session's list of spelling words and a sample sentence containing each trial word were included. In this fashion, the project director was confident that the tutors could verify all correct spelling attempts. Pronunciation of the words was practiced during a fifteen-minute period before each tutorial session. Deterline (1970) provides a very usable suggestion for insuring the tutor's being aware of the correct responses. An answer key, similar to that used by teachers in their daily classes, can provide the tutor with all of the correct responses. Some tutors will have little need of such answer sheets. For example, a ninth grader may be tutoring a second grader in basic math operations and be thoroughly familiar with the material. It is, however, a sound policy to provide tutors with an answer sheet so that they can sneak a look at it when they are uncertain of the correct response.

Another decision that the project director will make is who is to be responsible for scoring the materials during the sessions. In the last paragraph, we discussed providing scoring sheets to tutors. Some teachers ask the tutors to provide feedback to the tutee on the correctness of an answer, but also demand that the tutors not grade the lessons. This may be due to several reasons, first of which is that grading may be thought to be detrimental to the development of the tutee's self-confidence. The teacher may wish to use the information on the tutee's successes and failures to select and develop additional materials for that child. Other teachers have asked their tutors to indicate the number of trials it took the tutee to get the correct answer; but sometimes, the number of trials is not as important as the fact that the child being tutored finally got the answer right. The project director must clarify scoring procedures before the tutoring sessions begin.

Ehly (1975) describes how tutors were trained to follow specific procedures in correcting the tutee's answer and in recording the number of trials taken by the student to correctly spell each session's list of words. In this instance, the number of trials necessary for the student to spell each word correctly was not as important, for research purposes, as the amount of time each tutoring dyad required to complete a session.

When the scoring of the tutee's materials has been completed by each tutor during a session, some teachers review the answer sheets, looking for the deficiencies of individual students and checking on the accuracy of the tutor's scoring. When the child tutored is failing the majority of the lessons, and is not experiencing the success that is so critical to the development of a positive self-image, the teacher may decide to intervene in the tutoring process. The intervention may be to shorten the daily lesson, to provide more feedback on the tutee's performance, or to reward approximations of correct responses. In such instances, the teacher is striving to create an optimal situation for the tutee to learn. An alternative intervention is to assign a tutor who is experienced in working with students who are low achievers. Such a tutor will be beneficial to the child being tutored if he or she is warm, supportive, or otherwise capable of demonstrating acceptance of the tutee, no matter how that child is performing. Unconditional positive acceptance is one way of describing this quality in a tutor. A final alternative assignment for the child who is failing in the tutoring program is remedial tutoring arrangements. In such an arrangement, the student will be tutored on the basic concepts and techniques in a subject area. In many programs, there will be no need to designate tutoring sections as remedial or nonremedial. Students will be working at their own levels from the start. In other programs, the child who is not profiting from the sessions may be replaced by another student who has a greater likelihood of succeeding within the context of that program. For example, teachers may be facing a deadline when they will have their students take a nationally standardized test. If 75 percent of the students have the opportunity to receive tutoring on the content area of the test before it is given, then the teachers may decide to substitute a student from the remaining 25 percent when a previously selected student is not learning during the tutoring lessons. It is hoped that such a situation does not arise often in the schools. Peer tutoring can help all students if the time and energy can be given to developing a program to reach the individual child.

One way of monitoring the progress of the children being tutored is to test them on a regular basis during the program. This practice would supplement the information on the tutee's progress that is available on a daily basis from the tutor's logs and tutee's answer sheets. Testing enables the teacher to identify the student's areas of weakness, in addition to informing the child being tutored how he or she is progressing. If it is deemed necessary, the teacher may decide to meet with the tutor to discuss methods of increasing the tutee's performance in specific areas. This may be done by changing the content of the lessons or the processes by which materials are presented. In the latter instance, feedback from test results can assist the tutee to focus on what *has* been learned and what *remains* to be learned. When this feedback emphasizes the positive (that is, correct) responses, the child being tutored will be left with a feeling of accomplishment and success. The tutor then can discuss with the tutee what remains to be learned during the remaining sessions. It has been the authors' experience that frequent feedback to the children being tutored on their performance leads to a greater likelihood that these students will remember materials over the entire program at the termination of tutorial sessions. In one project, students were provided with daily feedback on their performance for that session. However, the students were not tested for retention of what they had learned until the end of the project (i.e., one month later). As a result, students were able to remember more of the content of the later sessions, but only a portion of the earlier ones. It would appear to be a good policy to test students regularly if only to monitor their progress.

Deterline (1970) makes the suggestion that when possible and appropriate, supplementary tests, similar in content area covered by any interim test, be developed by the teacher. Such a test can serve many purposes. First, it will test for generalization of whatever learning has taken place. Interim tests simply may reflect mastery of the more obvious elements of lesson content. Supplementary tests can give some indication of how soundly lesson concepts were grasped. Additionally, these tests provide practice in the lesson content and can serve as a remedial tool for any of the students who need extra time in which to learn lesson content.

A tutor record card can be developed for the tutor to record the performance on tests by the child being tutored. This card can be attached as part of the tutor's log.

A tutor assignment form also can be developed to serve as a record of the dates of tutoring, the name of the child who is being tutored (if this is a project that has a rotating assignment of tutors or an assignment-as-needed policy), and an indication of the tutee's status, vis-a-vis one unit in the tutorial program. The form can indicate the particular materials on which the tutee is working, the test for those materials, and the second test for that content, if such a test has been developed. By careful monitoring, a tutor who is called in to substitute for the regular tutor can begin at the point where instruction was terminated in the last session. Of course, this can only be accomplished when the lesson content is carefully structured and monitored. Regardless of whether a given program is highly structured, it is always a good policy to record what has been attempted in each session, i.e., what tests have been given by the tutor, and the performance of the tutee on the daily lesson and the tests. Such information can be recorded in the tutor's log if no other form is considered necessary by the project director.

In the above paragraphs some basic considerations in structuring a tutoring program have been presented. The topics considered have mentioned the content of the sessions without specifying how to choose or develop such content. While appropriate content is crucial to the success of peer tutoring projects, additional elements also must be acknowledged to manage a program efficiently.

CONSIDERATIONS AT THE EARLY STAGES OF A PROGRAM

The first few sessions in a tutoring program are crucial in establishing the expectancies for the participants and determining the "tone" that will carry throughout the remainder of the activities. These early sessions can be frustrating for the project director, participating teachers, and the students if there has been little or no previous planning as to the setting of specific responsibilities. We have discussed the absolute necessity of training tutors in appropriate instructional techniques and the scheduling of dyads on a stable basis. Additionally, it has been emphasized that consistent monitoring of progress is crucial to the success of a program. The project director can simplify the initial phases of the program by scheduling the tutorial pairs in specified rooms and insuring that these pairs are being monitored on a regular basis. When the pairs are not observed on a daily basis, the project coordinator can be responsible for determining the dates on which the pairs will be observed and who will be responsible for accomplishing the task. The centralized scheduling of all components of the program will alleviate much of the confusion that can result when too many people are trying to take charge in a program. This arrangement will make it easier for one person to discover the weaknesses in the ongoing operations of the program. For example, the project director may discover that a particular pair, who are not exhibiting satisfactory progress, are not meeting in the room to which they have been assigned. In this instance, the director should intervene to determine the reason for this breakdown in procedure. Appropriate action then can be taken, whether to find a better location or to deal with the problem of a tutor who is not meeting all of his or her responsibilities. This aspect of monitoring may highlight the deficiencies of a tutor in presenting materials on a prespecified schedule. Additional training may be indicated for certain tutors who are experiencing difficulty in fulfilling their duties.

From the authors' experience, the problems that result in the early stages of a tutorial program are usually not with the students fulfilling the requirements of their roles. Rather, the problems that occur result from *administrative* and *managerial* deficiencies. To illustrate, materials may not be immediately available, meeting times may be inappropriately scheduled, or the tutorial pairs may not be well suited to each other's particular strengths or weaknesses. When materials are not ready for a session, meeting spaces are scheduled for more than one dyad, or a test is not ready to give the children being tutored, the tutors may be left with no activities to carry out during the scheduled time. Such occurrences can have far-reaching implications. Children usually become frustrated if they are not allowed to fulfill their responsibilities. Conscientious attention must be maintained in all details of the tutorial project so that such mishaps don't occur. When an administrative goal is the *consistency* of arrangements throughout the duration of the project, sessions that take place as scheduled and in the planned manner should be the norm.

We have stressed the potential for collecting information on both partners in a tutoring relationship. This process is especially true during the early phases of a program. When efficient monitoring systems have been built into the management component of a tutoring project, the teacher or director will be provided a good indication of how well the tutor is doing. One problem frequently encountered is that certain tutors can overextend themselves in a tutoring relationship. When substantial planning is required by the tutor before each session, the tutor may find increasingly less time to devote to classroom studies or extracurricular activities. When this occurs, the tutor may neglect to inform his or her teacher of the pressures created by participating in the tutoring project. The ongoing process of monitoring can uncover a tutor's difficulties in these areas. Another method of identifying undue pressures on the tutor involves the project director maintaining contact with the tutor's teacher or teachers, so that they can report on observable positive or negative changes in the student's behavior.

Deterline (1970) suggests that when project staff differs from the children's teachers, all parties should meet to discuss the progress of the tutees in the program. The child's teacher can suggest additional areas in which the tutee can work, or request remedial intervention in a particular area. Contact between project and classroom staff also serves to keep everyone informed of what the student is doing in each setting. Feedback on the successes of a child in a tutorial program can be a powerful force in modifying a teacher's attitudes towards a student who had previously experienced only failure in the classroom.

THE TUTOR'S ROLE IN PRESENTING MATERIALS

In Chapter III, we discussed the responsibilities of the tutor and the importance of training him/her in meeting these responsibilities. We considered information from several sources on the expectations set for tutors in several programs. It would be helpful in this section to review the variety of requirements that can be placed on the tutor in terms of presenting materials to the tutee.

Deterline (1970) succinctly described the tutor's function: "The tutor, given a question, problem, or task previously performed incorrectly by the tutee, will, through a series of questions, help the tutee arrive at and practice the correct answer." This definition reflects the process of many tutoring programs. Other programs place less emphasis on the questioning process, with the tutors following a prespecified program of presenting materials. The tutor remains the agent who delivers the materials to the partner.

Another important responsibility for the tutor is providing feedback and, when appropriate, rewards for the tutee's response. The tutor can provide examples of problem-solving or other prompting devices that are advisable within the context of the program. A further responsibility is for the tutor to maintain a positive and helpful attitude at all times. It surely will not hurt if the child being tutored believes that the tutor is enjoying the tutoring session! The tutor can model a positive and confident stance towards the solving of academic problems.

An additional tutor responsibility can be assigned by the project director or the participating teachers if considered desirable. This responsibility involves the development and construction of materials for the tutorial sessions. In some projects, such as the Youth Tutoring Youth project, tutors assumed primary responsibility in creating materials. Indeed, the project's directors have attributed, in part, the gains experienced by the tutors to this aspect of the program. In other projects, the tutors have a minimal role in developing materials. Their role may be simply to inform the teacher when additional materials are needed.

STRUCTURING MATERIALS BY THE TUTOR

The learning process in the classroom is similar in many ways to what is going on in the tutoring sessions. The largest differences relate to the individual attention afforded the learner in the tutoring context. For the tutoring experience to meet most effectively the academic and affective needs of the child being tutored, the tutor can be given responsibility for matching materials to the needs of the student at the time of the session.

Cohen, Kirk, and Dickson (1972) have discussed at length the structuring of materials in the tutorial setting. Cohen and his colleagues stressed the immediacy of the tutoring experience and the fact that it allows for an accurate reading of the progress of the child being tutored. The authors suggest a five-point strategy for the use and structuring of materials in tutoring. The five points are:

1   diagnosing the learner's difficulty,
2   determining the specific problem areas of the tutee, whether academic or social-emotional,
3   focusing on the strong points, cognitive and affective, of the child being tutored,
4   relating the content and materials to the work being done in the classroom, and
5   relating the materials to the interests of the child being tutored.

Considering the aspect of diagnosis, the teacher and the tutor, whether responsible for the development of materials or not, should approach the tutoring session with the goal of specifying the strengths and weaknesses of the tutee. The strengths and weaknesses may be in academic areas or may reflect the social-emotional status of the student being tutored. Following naturally from the diagnostic phase will be the establishment of goals and objectives pertinent to the individual student. The goals and objectives should permit the specification of *terminal behaviors* expected of the tutee, as well as those daily activities that are considered necessary to accomplish the interim goals. Obviously, it is essential to state both long- and short-term goals and objectives for both academic and social areas in order to insure consistent presentation by the tutor and mastery by the tutee.

Once the tutee's strengths and weaknesses have been identified, the teacher *or* tutor must begin to examine the materials to be used during the tutoring sessions. It is not uncommon to find that some students may be capable of grasping a certain concept, but do not because of difficulties in working with the certain curricular materials that are designed to teach that concept. When the tutee appears to be exhibiting difficulty working with particular types of materials, plans should be made to utilize other modes of presenting information within the tutorial context. A decision may be made to assist the tutee in coping with more difficult and advanced material presentations. Examination of the tutee's performance in the regular classroom may reveal that certain students perform poorly when tested in a particular format, e.g., in essay style. Provided with this information, test materials can be structured so that the tutee will have a greater likelihood of experiencing success within the regular classroom.

Observing the tutee in the classroom also can provide many clues as to what does and does not work instructionally with the tutee. The purpose of the observation is to determine the most appropriate manner of presenting content to the student, as well as the most beneficial type of materials to use. To illustrate, the tutee may be seen to sit passively in his chair when he is given a worksheet to complete. With this bit of information, the program director may plan activities to assist the tutee in becoming more actively involved with the tutor by means of requiring the child to respond at frequent intervals to content when it is presented.

In addition to focusing upon the deficiencies of the tutee, the observer should note the strengths of the child. A pupil's strengths provide an optimal entry point in initial tutorial activities. With this information, the tutor will be able to provide immediate success to the tutee by concentrating on that child's areas of demonstrated knowledge. Affective strengths can be used to "hook" the tutee into the tutoring process. For example, if the tutee prides him/herself on being accurate, the tutor can stress the importance of being accurate with the answer to a particular worksheet. By being reinforced for existing positive habits, the child will be more likely to enjoy and work at the materials than would be the case if the child received no such reinforcement. With the extensive information that can be provided by the careful observation of the child, the director's responsibilities of setting objectives and specifying materials for the tutee will be simplified.

The second point to consider when structuring materials in tutoring is determining the degree of activity required by the tutee. Cohen and his colleagues (1972) have stressed the importance of the active participation of the tutee in the program's activities. The tutee should be expected to do something at all times, whether that be reading, listening, writing, or working on a problem. The more active the tutee, the more information that will be available to the tutor and the teacher on the child's academic and social-emotional status. It has been demonstrated that the tutee is more likely to learn when he or she is active rather than passively watching the tutor during the sessions (Cohen et al., 1972).

The task of keeping the tutee active requires a well-trained tutor and extensive programming of materials that are varied, of interest, and relevant to the tutee. The creative imagination of the professional who programs materials will be tested in developing materials that contain meaningful intent as well as being stimulating. One illustration of a teacher's creative response to the needs of tutoring a child is that of Mrs. Wolfe and her student, Charles. Charles, a second grader, not only was resistant to reading the lowest basal reader, he believed he was incapable of reading at all. When assigned an understanding and perceptive tutor, Charles revealed that he would "read" along with his father as he read bedtime stories. The teacher located Charles' favorite stories and the tutor used these as the texts for instruction. Charles was able to recognize many of the words in the stories. The tutor auditorially recorded the sessions so that Charles could hear himself reading. After several sessions, Charles exhibited such pride in his new-found reading abilities that he begged his teacher to let him read to her.

In reading, math, and other subjects there is a wealth of high-interest, low-ability materials available commercially that can be used with the tutee who has specific academic deficiencies. These materials are expensive but have long-term benefits for the child who would not have been reached otherwise. Special-interest magazines, newspapers, comic books, and story books are additional sources of content material for the tutee. An advantage of these materials is that they are familiar and of interest to the tutee and the tutor.

As discussed, the third important point when structuring materials for a tutoring program is emphasizing the strong points, both cognitive and affective, of the child being tutored. The importance of this strategy lies in providing success experiences for the child who is likely to be discouraged with the learning process and may have been "tuning out" the teacher in the regular classroom. With success, greater enthusiasm for learning will be frequently exhibited. This enthusiasm will translate to the regular classroom when the teacher is kept well-informed of what instructional activities will be most beneficial when used with the tutee.

The fourth point to consider when structuring tutorial materials is relating the content and materials to the work being done in the student's classroom. Obviously, the program director would not want to present the tutee content that is unrelated to classroom activities.

The more similar the concepts being presented in the classroom *and* the tutorial sessions, the more likely that any transition of acquired skill back into the classroom will be successful. Similarity in the material used in the classroom and the tutorial sessions works to the tutee's advantage. It is possible to use materials identical to those employed in the classroom, or, when introducing new materials or ways of presenting materials, to insure that the classroom teacher is kept informed and is assisted in utilizing these materials if desired.

The importance of consistency in the scheduling of tutorial sessions applies to the programming of materials. Materials that are consistent in scope and style with classroom norms can help the tutee to settle into the requirements of the tutorial program quickly. Consistency of materials across tutorial sessions is important and enables the tutee to develop sets and expectations for working on the presented materials. The tutor must play an important role in establishing a set pattern during sessions by maintaining contact with the program director and insuring that the material is appropriate to the established needs of the tutee.

The final point to keep in mind when structuring materials for tutoring is relating the materials to the interests of the child being tutored. When possible, the voiced interests of the child will provide valuable insights. Such topics as sports have proven to be favorites of both boys and girls. Hobbies, pets, and television shows are also of high interest to children. Using the already mentioned high-interest, low-vocabulary materials available from many educational materials companies is one avenue of reaching the older child who is not learning in the classroom. A tutee's interest in such topics as stunt motorcycling can be used to the child's advantage when materials on this topic are used as tutorial content. Of course, for these materials to be used easily by the pupil, they must be geared to an appropriate reading level.

One example of using a tutee's demonstrated interest to promote effective classroom learning was evidenced in the case of a child labeled "retarded" by his teacher. The child was observed to be doodling on a worksheet in class. When the teacher noticed that the boy had drawn an accurate presentation of the Star Ship Enterprise, he approached the boy about his interest in the Star Trek series. The child was highly conversant with all the characters and events in this TV series. By coincidence, this student was engaged in a tutoring project but was demonstrating no apparent progress. The teacher became excited with the possibility of designing program materials with a Star Trek theme. Very quickly, the tutoring sessions, utilizing the new materials, took a turn that delighted the tutor, tutee and teacher. The tutee was completing arithmetic problems and reading assignments that related to events aboard the Enterprise. The tutor enjoyed his work more and volunteered to help the teacher develop materials for the tutorial sessions. The teacher continued the high-interest materials in the classroom when the tutorial sessions were completed.

In summary, it is apparent that program content must remain interesting to the tutee throughout the sessions in order to maintain the student's attention. Even an interest in Star Trek can wear out when the focus remains on this single theme. Variety in themes and types of materials will help keep the tutee interested and willing to remain on task. It should be noted that instructional games can be a learning device for children. The tutor is likely to have ideas on games and other materials that will be of interest to the tutee.

As developed by Ellson and his colleagues (1965), programmed tutoring is a potential alternative to the structuring of materials. The programming process involves a high degree of structure. The Ellson approach was developed with tutors who were parent volunteers and other adults. College and high school students also have worked with the process. The interested reader will find much information available regarding programmed tutoring. Ellson, Harris and Barber (1968) provide an outline that specifies the procedure for developing materials appropriate for programmed tutoring activities.

CONSTRUCTING MATERIALS FOR THE PEER TUTORING PROGRAM

When materials for peer tutoring programming are not already available from a project with similar objectives or from the educational marketplace, the program director will be faced with the development of materials that can meet the needs of a tutee's stated objectives. (The mention of materials from the educational marketplace refers to the existence of "canned" tutorial programs. Rather than discuss the specific merits or weaknesses of these materials, the authors suggest that the reader solicit such product information from educational publishing companies.) Following the decision that constructing materials is necessary, it is then imperative to determine who will be responsible for developing the materials. Teachers, aides, student volunteers, and tutors are all candidates to handle this task.

The creation of tutorial materials need not be burdensome to the teacher or the project director. When a smattering of materials is appropriate for use in a given program, it must be determined whether to modify the materials to reflect more accurately the goals of the program and the needs of the students. Goals and needs of the tutee at his or her most basic level affect the decision of which materials to select and use. For example, if the teacher would like the tutee to master the materials in a particular reader, that book would be the logical choice for the content of the tutorial academics. However, in situations where the student is not able to master the contents of a book, simply placing the student in tutorials with the same book may not be an appropriate decision. The pupil may be capable of acquiring the concepts in the reader but not possess the necessary skills to actually decode the words. The teacher must then structure activities to assist the student in acquiring essential skills. If all goes well, the tutee, through the use of supplementary materials such as crossword puzzles or high-interest worksheets, will be able to master basic skills necessary to meet established goals. The decision to try tutoring with such students may reflect the teacher's desire to give that child more individual attention without drawing him or her away from other classroom activities and demands.

The child who is having great difficulty acquiring the concepts in the reader or, more basically, being able to read the words in the book, may not profit as much by high-interest materials as by the intensive attention that tutoring directs to his or her academic deficits. The tutor can work with such a child to provide a better grounding in prerequisite skills necessary for acquisition of the concepts in the reader. This may be done by using a lower-level reader (one that can be at a lower grade level) as the tutorial content. This reader can be supplemented with other materials that also reflect the skills to be learned in that book. The tutoring arrangements will allow the child to receive remedial academics as well as the personalized learning that tutoring permits.

Modifying existing materials can be accomplished in several ways, all of which must result in meeting the needs and objectives of the tutee. In identifying materials to meet the academic objectives of the child, the teacher will be matching the content to the specific learning objectives for that student or group of students. To illustrate, the teacher who would like the tutee to acquire competency in spelling words at grade level would utilize spelling lists or texts which focus on words at this ability level, as well as such materials that would serve to reinforce the learning of such words. The word lists used may be locally developed or simply taken from the spelling series used in the regular classroom. Other academic areas, such as social studies, may not be as easily translated to the tutorial style as would spelling materials. However, existing materials on this subject could be modified to teach the particular concepts contained in the students' objectives.

The teacher who has a previously developed collection of materials focusing on the affective needs of the tutee is fortunate indeed. There are very few programs that have been directed exclusively at meeting affective objectives for the child being tutored. When materials are available, they should be examined in view of the specific objectives for the students in the program. The majority of tutorial programs emphasize the affective domains not so much in the content of their materials, but rather in the techniques of relating to the children and the methods they use to present those materials. Programs that have used affectively-oriented materials with their students have reported that children in both the tutor and tutee roles benefit from and enjoy such content. Programs such as Youth Tutoring Youth delegate the development of affective materials to the tutors involved in the project.

An example of the content of affective materials that can be used in the tutorial context is provided by a program located in the Southwestern region of the United States. Teachers in this program had developed a variety of materials that were affective in their orientation. Their approach was refined to the point that they merely had to identify the affective needs of their students and select materials from their tutorial files that were designed to meet the particular needs. The child who was shy and passive in class would be matched with a tutor who had been trained to work with unresponsive children. The materials emphasized the involvement of the tutee in the learning task, which dealt in part with social situations that would elicit the participation of a typical bystander. A high degree of variety was present in the materials, further drawing the student into the ongoing processes of the tutorial sessions.

The comments in the preceding paragraphs have reflected the situation in which materials are available to use in the tutoring program. These materials may have been clearly identified as tutorial materials. The teacher about to develop a tutoring program in his or her classroom normally will not have such resources on hand. Materials will have to be developed. However, our considerations on modifying materials are valid also. The selection of materials will be influenced both by the learning and affective objectives set for the students and the tutorial approach emphasized in the program. Regarding this latter point, the selection of materials for a programmed tutoring project may differ from those selected for a peer tutoring program. The selection of materials will, in part, be determined by the ability of the tutors to administer them in an appropriate manner. Moreover, the differences in approach probably would not result in the selection of differing materials but rather in the structuring of any materials to adapt to the context of the ongoing sessions.

Matching materials to objectives requires both the specification of objectives, whether academic or affective, and the identification of materials to meet such objectives. The materials may already be available in the classroom. Textbooks, worksheets, and educational games may be the materials that the teacher would like the student to master. In these instances, the teacher can shape the materials into lessons that the tutor merely would have to present to the tutee. However, modification of materials may be necessary so that the materials can be successfully used in a tutorial context. For example, a worksheet may have been developed in social studies for the entire class working as a group. This worksheet could be altered to shift the response requirements from the group level to the individual level.

Materials designed to meet the affective goals in a program may be developed at the local school level. Materials may be found in the classroom that could be used to meet these objectives. Content suggestions may occur to the teacher who has used an affective program previously. Examples of such programs are Magic Circle and DUSO (i.e., Developing Understanding of Self and Others). The themes of these programs' lessons can be incorporated into the content of the lessons.

Both affective and academic materials may not be available in a single classroom to meet the requirements of a tutorial program. The tutorial program that involves several classrooms in a cooperative tutorial effort is at a distinct advantage. In a cross-age tutorial program, teachers in the lower grades can contribute remedial materials at the lower grade level to teachers who will be working with older, underachieving students. Supplementary tutorial materials may be provided by parents who are interested in helping to establish a tutorial program. These materials may consist of games, puzzles, magazines, and comic books. These materials can be utilized as is in the tutoring sessions, or may be placed within a more structured context. Whatever materials are used, they should reflect the goals of the program and should meet the learning and affective objectives set for the students.

The discussion of materials thus far has focused primarily upon educational objectives delineated for the tutee. Meeting the academic and affective objectives set for the *tutor* usually is secondary to those of the tutee. In those cases where tutor objectives are of primary concern, materials will not be modified extensively to meet the tutor's academic needs. Rather, the experience of working as a tutor and being able to learn by reviewing and reformulating the lesson content will probably result in learning gains for the tutor. Affectively-oriented materials may be shaped to meet the tutor's objectives in a variety of ways. For example, the student who has been isolated from his peer group can be given a tutor assignment that requires him to work closely with a classmate. The structuring of the content will result in a much higher level of involvement with peers. Content materials additionally could deal with themes of group identity and belongingness.

Teacher or Student Development of Materials?

The generation of ideas for materials to use in the tutoring program can involve all participants, teachers, tutors, and tutees. In order to facilitate the process, program directors or classroom teachers should solicit the reactions of the students to already-existing materials, as well as the students' suggestions for additional materials. The responsibility for the development or acquisition of new materials can be shared by teachers and students or delegated to other professional personnel.

Many teachers are most comfortable when they retain the sole responsibility for the creation of program materials. This desire usually stems from the feeling that in maintaining this control, they can develop lesson plans for the sessions that can meet in an optimal manner the objectives that they have created for their students. And, indeed, materials developed by teachers do tend to be neater, more structured, and more precise than the materials developed by students.

Tutors and other students have been recruited in many tutoring projects to create new and supplementary materials for the program. The students may be asked to make stencils of existing materials or copies of recently acquired materials. Oftentimes, the students will bring to school books and games that they believe could be used effectively in tutoring their partner. In a few projects, the tutors have been given the responsibility for defining what materials they will use during the sessions.

The teacher or project director might profitably decide to use a combination of both teacher- and student-made materials. When students do participate in this task, they should be well informed of the specific requirements necessary to develop appropriate materials. This can be done by outlining for the tutor the objectives for the tutee and the criteria that adopted materials must meet, such as length, difficulty, and mode of presentation. The teacher should be detailed in providing the tutors with information on objectives and adoption criteria. By doing so, the teacher is likely to be presented with materials that will meet the guidelines established. The teacher may wish to review all student-made materials before using them, so that poorly made or inappropriate materials can be eliminated.

The Presentation of Content Materials

The manner in which materials can be presented to the tutee varies with types of materials used and the philosophy of the program. Materials will be structured so that they can be presented in the one-to-one context of the tutorial situation. Some materials will be more amenable than others to this method of presentation. For example, some materials readily can be reduced into smaller units to fit the time guidelines of a program. The program's philosophy can determine the amount of structure attached to the presentation of materials or the emphasis placed on the active participation of the students.

When such considerations have been made by the program director, work can proceed on structuring the content of the sessions. The structure may be minimal. Tutors may have a large degree of freedom in how they present the lesson to their partners. The other extreme is that of tutors being required to present all materials in a predetermined manner. An example of this can be instances in which programmed tutoring is used in the tutorial project. Another example is the situation in which research demands will not allow for any variations in the presentation of materials. We have discussed such a project in spelling.

More likely will be those instances in which the project director has trained the tutors to follow certain guidelines in the presentation of materials, allowing for variations to be introduced by the tutors to meet situational needs. One method of specifying the manner of presenting materials lies in the use of lesson plans. With a lesson plan in hand, the tutor is able to present materials in the proper sequence and in predetermined amounts. The teacher who uses lesson plans is able to maintain records of what has been covered in the sessions, as well as the presentation methods used. Feedback on the tutee's use of materials with each method can be used by the teacher to shape future lessons, as well as to modify classroom techniques of working with the student. Cohen, Kirk and Dickson (1972) have presented a series of chapters on structuring the content of reading, math, and social studies for a tutorial program. Their suggestions will be especially helpful to the teacher who wants to develop a tutoring program with bilingual children. Sample lesson plans for a tutoring program are attached as an addendum to this chapter (see Addendum 5A).

Techniques Contingent on Content Decisions

There are two considerations that can follow the decision of which materials to use during the tutoring sessions. These are the use of a reinforcement system and the use of a contract system. The decision to use a reinforcement system in a program may reflect the belief in the usefulness of such a system or may be an existing component of the program that is being conducted. Rewarding the students for their responses or their attending to task can be effective in maintaining or increasing the response rate of students. Tutors will reward their partners both verbally and nonverbally, whether there is a defined reward system or not. When there is a definite reinforcement system, the project director must decide both how often and when to assign rewards. The next decision is what type of rewards to use. When these decisions have been made, it is important to define as specifically as possible for the tutors the reinforcement schedule and reward techniques of the program.

Contracting for the completion of materials can be an important and useful technique in a tutoring program. The reader may be familiar already with contracting systems. Tutees meet with their partners or with their teachers to establish goals for the completion of materials or for the meeting of behavioral or affective criteria. The contracts may have an attached reinforcement system. Teachers in several tutoring programs have contracted with the tutors on the completion of behavioral and work goals for sessions. Contracting can help the students to become more sensitive to the demands that are being placed on them in the tutoring program.

Monitoring and Evaluating Content

The need to monitor the implementation of the components of a tutorial program applies in the content area also. Whether by teacher observations or tutor self-checks, the monitoring of what materials are being used, and in what manner, will fall to the project director and others who have assumed the responsibility for the program's operations. Monitoring tutors on use of content materials not only will insure that the appropriate materials are being used correctly, but will give valuable feedback on the demands placed by the content procedures on the tutor and the tutee. With this feedback, future materials can be modified to be more readily administered or more appropriate to the students' objectives.

Few programs formally evaluate the content of their tutorial program. Rather, programs informally assess the fit of materials to objectives, and the ease with which students can teach each other using the materials. Process methods of evaluation allow the teacher to evaluate both the content of the sessions and the procedures employed to present the materials. An example of evaluating the content of a program would be to have participating teachers and tutors rate the usefulness of the materials as well as the feasibility of applying these materials in other tutoring programs. A similar approach can be taken to evaluate the usefulness and feasibility of content procedures. In addition, participants may rate the feasibility of using tutorial content and procedures in the regular classroom.

Product evaluation of content refers to the post-tutorial measures that are given to determine the acquisition of tutorial content by the tutee and, less often, by the tutor. Product evaluation will inform the teacher simply whether the students have reached their objectives or have not. Product and process information on content will guide the teacher in making content and procedural changes in future sessions or programs.

Addendum 5A
SAMPLE LESSON PLANS

Tutee:	Jeff
Grade:	Kindergarten
Subject:	Math
Tutor:	Ronnie

TUTEE'S CASE DESCRIPTION

Family Background

Jeff is a five-year-old male who is currently enrolled in kindergarten. Until December Jeff was the only child in his family; a sister has recently been added to his family. In a recent conference, Jeff's mother stated that since the birth of his sister Jeff has become very uncooperative at home. She remarked, "Jeff refuses to follow our directions. If he is asked to play quietly so that he won't disturb the baby, Jeff deliberately makes loud noises." She also noted that Jeff frequently requests to remain at home rather than go to school and cries when he is told that he must go to kindergarten.

Academic Background

In the kindergarten classroom Jeff has difficulty in cooperating with his teacher, Miss Matthews, and his classmates. Jeff does not complete his school assignments and has difficulty in remaining at his assigned table. The kindergarten teacher has also noticed that since the arrival of his sister, Jeff demands increasingly more individual attention from her. Jeff also complains that he doesn't enjoy school and frequently requests to be sent home.

Rationale for Initiating Peer Tutoring

Although Jeff's academic performance is adequate in the content areas of reading, handwriting, and oral language, he is experiencing difficulty in mathematics. Jeff is unable to recognize the numerals 5-10 and to count from 1-10. Since the kindergarten classroom is very large this year, Miss Matthews doesn't feel that she will be able to give Jeff the individual teaching sessions that would cover his special problems within the math area. However, Miss Matthews realizes that Jeff really needs more individual attention at this particular time. Therefore, Jeff's teacher has decided to initiate a cross-age peer tutoring program which will give Jeff not only remedial work in math, but also the individual attention that he seems to need. Ronnie, a fourth grade student, will conduct daily tutoring sessions with Jeff. The peer tutoring sessions will be continued for three weeks.

SPECIFIC OBJECTIVES AND ACTIVITIES FOR PEER TUTORING

General Objectives

1 Jeff should develop recognition of numerals.
2 Jeff should be able to count in proper sequential order.
3 Jeff should develop the ability to work independently.

Specific Objectives*

1 Jeff should recognize the numerals 5, 6, 7.
2 Jeff should understand the numerical concept of 5, 6, 7.
3 Jeff should count in sequential order from 1-7.
4 Jeff should complete the work that his tutor assigns.

Suggested Activities

1 The tutor places a tree, 10 leaves, and the numerals 1-7 on the felt board. The tutor asks Jeff to place a certain number of leaves on the tree using the numerals 5, 6, 7. Jeff then chooses the felt numeral that corresponds with the number of leaves on the tree.
2 The tutor asks Jeff to insert the appropriate number of pegs into the wooden number line that corresponds with the numeral at the top.
3 The tutor places felt numerals from 1-7 on the felt board in sequential order and says each numeral aloud as he does this. Jeff says the numeral aloud with his tutor, pointing to each numeral as he says it. Jeff places a set of felt numerals identical to the tutor's row on the felt board, counting aloud as he does this.

*The specific objective may also contain an evaluation measure as included under the evaluation section of this lesson plan.

4 Using a toy train set which has a numeral taped on each car, Jeff hooks the cars together in correct numerical order.
5 After the tutor has given the necessary directions, Jeff independently completes a math worksheet that consists of counting sets of objects from 1-7.
6 After Jeff's tutor has given directions, Jeff independently completes a page in his math book on counting from 1-10.

Materials

1 Felt board
2 Felt numerals 1-7
3 Ten felt leaves
4 Wooden number lines
5 Pegs
6 Toy train set
7 Number cans
8 Tongue depressors
9 Worksheet
10 Jeff's math book

Evaluation

The evaluation of Jeff's peer tutoring program will be conducted immediately following the three weeks of daily tutoring sessions.

1 Jeff should place the appropriate number of tongue depressors in cans with the numerals from 1-7 on the can with 100 percent accuracy. Jeff should then place the cans in correct numerical order.
2 Jeff should count the number of objects in eight separate boxes which will not contain over seven objects and place the numeral which corresponds to the number of objects in front of each box with 90 percent accuracy.
3 Jeff should place the numerals 1-7 in correct numerical order.

Tutor's Comments

Tutee:	Trina
Grade:	2
Subject:	Reading
Tutor:	Mary

TUTEE'S CASE DESCRIPTION

Family Background

Trina is a seven-year-old female who is presently in the third month of second grade. A younger sister, Ellen, is Trina's only sibling. Both girls live with their mother. Currently Trina's parents are separated and the father resides in another state. At the beginning of school, Trina's mother talked with the classroom teacher and expressed concern over Trina's "lack of responsibility." During the conference she stated, "Trina never listens; she just doesn't follow directions." Upon questioning Trina's mother further, the teacher learned that a physician had checked Trina's hearing and could find no medical difficulties. An additional concern of Trina's mother was the academic competition that was occurring between her two daughters, especially in the area of reading. She commented, "Ellen is only starting first grade and she can read almost as well as Trina. Trina refuses to read aloud when Ellen is present." Before ending the conference, Trina's mother did say that she felt that Trina enjoyed school and was very excited about the prospect of second grade.

Academic Background

In the school setting Trina has been described by her teacher as a very cooperative and enthusiastic student. Trina's teacher notes, "Trina is continuously concerned with the quality of her school performance. Trina does, however, have great difficulty in following directions and generally she requires individual directions on each assignment, especially those in her reading workbook." The teacher also commented that Trina has difficulty in retelling a personal experience or the story of a show that she saw on television. Trina is also experiencing difficulty in completing her reading assignments. She has many problems in comprehending what she has read. Trina's inability to follow directions causes some problems on the school playground. The other children frequently complain that Trina can't remember how to play certain games. In spite of her peers' complaints, Trina is always eager to participate in classroom activities.

Rationale for Initiating Peer Tutoring

Trina is progressing at an average rate in the content area of handwriting and spelling. Trina does not, however, remember the basic addition and subtraction facts through 20. In the content area of reading, Trina displays adequate skills in decoding new words through the usage of phonetic elements; comprehension of the reading material presents a problem. Trina does well with most questions that involve simple recall such as names of characters, main events, and specific details, but she has problems with inferential comprehension such as interpretation of cause and effect, inferences, and temporal sequence of the story. Since Trina is always very cooperative and does need individual attention, the second grade teacher is recommending Trina for a peer tutoring program which will continue on a daily basis for a period of one month. The tutoring program will focus on following directions and temporal sequencing in reading. At the end of one month the tutoring will be evaluated to determine if additional tutoring sessions would be beneficial for Trina.

General Objectives

1 Trina should develop the ability to following directions.
2 Trina should improve the quality of her inferential comprehension skills in reading.
3 Trina should develop awareness of temporal sequence.

Specific Objectives

1 When given three directions by the tutor, Trina should follow the directions in the correct sequence.
2 Trina should sequence pictures so that they tell a story.
3 Trina should be given a set of sequenced pictures and tell a story about the pictures in proper sequence.
4 After listening to a story, Trina should retell the story in its proper sequence.
5 After reading a story silently, Trina should retell the story in its proper sequence.
6 Trina should follow the directions given by her tutor.

Suggested Activities—Phase I

1 The tutor verbally gives Trina three directions at one time, and Trina follows the directions in the order that they are given, e.g.:
   a Walk to the door, close the door and return to your desk.
   b Close your book, put your pencil in your desk and stand beside your chair.
   c Put your pencil on the desk, get your reading book and return to page 46.
2 The tutor gives Trina worksheets which contain directions commonly used in workbooks that are to be followed. The tutor helps Trina complete these worksheets.
3 On a sheet of writing paper Trina lists in sequence her daily activities such as getting ready for school, the daily school routine, getting ready for bed, etc.
4 The tutor asks Trina questions concerning a set of pictures that form a story, stressing what happens first and last; Trina then sequences the pictures so that they tell the story in proper order.
5 As an art activity, Trina illustrates common sequences in our environment such as the seasons or special holidays.

Suggested Activities—Phase II

6 The tutor reads a story to Trina and then asks questions about what happened first and last in the story.
7 The tutor reads a story to Trina and then asks questions pertaining to the order that events occurred in the story. After discussing the story, Trina retells the story to the teacher.
8 Trina reads silently a story from her reading book and tells the tutor what occurred first and last in the story.
9 Trina reads a story silently from her basal reader and retells the story to her tutor in its proper sequence.
10 The tutor and Trina read a story together and discuss what they have read. The tutor gives Trina four sentences or sentence strips describing events from the story. Trina places the sentences in the order that they occurred in the story.

Materials

1 Worksheets prepared by teacher
2 Sets of pictures that form stories

3 Crayons
4 Paper
5 Trina's reading book
6 Library books to be read by tutor

Evaluation

Evaluation will be conducted twice during the duration of the peer tutoring program. The first evaluation will occur at the end of the first two weeks. The second evalution will be at the completion of the peer tutoring program.

Evaluation I.

1 Trina should complete a worksheet on following written directions with 100 percent accuracy.
2 Trina should follow three verbal directions given together with 100 percent accuracy.
3 Trina should arrange a set of pictures into the proper sequence and tell a story about the pictures.

Evaluation II.

1 Trina should listen to a story and answer questions concerning the sequence of events in the story with 90 percent accuracy.
2 Trina should listen to a story and then arrange a set of pictures about the story in the order of their occurrence in the story with 100 percent accuracy.
3 Trina should read a story silently and tell what happened first and last in the story with 100 percent accuracy.
4 Trina should read a story silently and then number four sentences describing events from the story in the order that they occurred in the story.

Tutor's Comments

Tutee:	Randy
Grade:	5
Subject:	Spelling
Tutor:	Mark

TUTEE'S CASE DESCRIPTION

Family Background

Randy is a new student in the fifth grade classroom who has recently transferred from a much smaller school in another state. Randy is the youngest of three boys; all of the siblings presently live with their parents. Since Randy is on a lower academic level than the other students in his new room, his teacher, Mrs. Jones, felt that Randy's parents should be aware of his school problem. However, the parents did not show up for the first two appointments Mrs. Jones had scheduled with them. During the conference neither parent displayed any observable concern over Randy's academic functioning. The mother's remarks were "Randy is just all boy." The father comments, "Well, I didn't do very well in school myself." Randy is frequently absent and his teacher suspects that he may occasionally be absent without a substantial reason.

Academic Background

Although Randy is a new student, he has formed friendships with his peers very quickly. He appears to get along very well with the other students. Since Randy excels in all areas of sports, he is a favorite among the boys. Randy is very proud of his physical abilities and frequently boasts about his successes. However, Randy appears to be very unhappy in the academic setting of the classroom. Randy is performing two years below grade level on all academic subjects. Whenever Randy is required to do any assignments that require written expression, he complains that the work is too hard and that he can't do it. Generally, Randy does not complete his assignments and he never returns homework assignments. After examining Randy's work requiring written expression, his teacher noticed that Randy's major mistakes were in spelling. There were numerous misspelled words including basic sight words on all of Randy's assignments that required written expression. On Randy's last report card the teacher stated, "Due to Randy's academic problems, school has become a very frustrating situation for him. I am quite concerned about Randy's attitude toward the school environment." Randy's teacher has referred Randy to the school counselor so that he may receive additional help from other educational sources.

Rationale for Initiating Peer Tutoring

Even though Randy has been referred for additional educational services, the fifth grade teacher feels he needs help immediately. Since Randy relates well with the other students, it is the teacher's opinion that a peer tutoring program could be beneficial to him. Since spelling poses a major problem in all of Randy's written assignments, this would be a good content area for additional help. After conducting an informal spelling assessment, Mrs. Jones has determined that Randy needs to begin work at the second grade level. Mrs. Jones also believes that if Randy has more success in the academic areas, then perhaps he will attend school more often. Therefore, Randy will be involved in a peer tutoring program daily for a period of five weeks. Randy's spelling program will be taken from a second grade spelling book.

General Objectives

1 Randy's daily attendance should increase.
2 Randy should improve the quality of his spelling skills.

Specific Objectives

1 Randy should attend 90 percent of his tutoring sessions.
2 Randy should correctly spell 10 new words each week.
3 Randy should form a sentence using each of the spelling words.

Suggested Activities

1 The tutor gives Randy a pretest at the beginning of each week which consists of 10 words from the spelling book on second grade level. The tutor checks the test to determine which words Randy will study during that week.
2 Randy copies all 10 spelling words on 3 X 5 cards. He takes home the words that he has not mastered; the words he can spell correctly may be placed in his *Words I Know* file.

3 Randy traces each word card three times and then writes the word from memory on the chalkboard. Randy checks his own work by referring to his word card.

4 The tutor directs Randy in forming sentences using each of his spelling words. Randy then copies the sentences on paper.

5 The tutor prepares a worksheet with missing words that Randy reads; he completes the sheet using his spelling words.

6 Randy unscrambles felt letters on the felt board to form his weekly spelling words.

Materials

1 Spelling book—grade 2
2 3 X 5 index cards—unlined
3 File box
4 Worksheets
5 Felt letters
6 Felt board

Evaluation

Evaluation will be conducted at the end of each week during the weekly spelling lists. At the end of the five-week period, a composite spelling test will be administered. Also Randy's tutor will keep a daily log of attendance to determine if Randy attended 90 percent of the sessions.

1 Randy should spell with 80 percent accuracy his weekly list of spelling words.

2 Randy should form a sentence using each of the weekly spelling words with 90 percent accuracy.

Tutor's Comments

Tutee:	Bryan
Grade:	8
Subject:	Written Expression
Tutor:	Mike

TUTEE'S CASE DESCRIPTION

Family Background

Bryan, a boy in the eighth grade, has just returned to public school after being in a homebound school program for the past eight months. Bryan suffered several injuries in a car accident that made it impossible for him to attend regular school classes. Bryan is in good physical condition, but he is much smaller than the other boys; he also walks with a pronounced limp which makes it impossible for him to participate in physical activities. Bryan is a very quiet child. Bryan's parents are very concerned that he may encounter difficulty in making new friends. They feel that Bryan's limp causes him to feel very embarrassed and insecure around his peers. Although they continuously urge Bryan to bring friends home after school, he says that he doesn't have any friends. The mother says that Bryan spends the majority of his free time after school building models or playing with his dog. During a conference with the school counselor, she remarked "Bryan is a very responsible and cooperative child, but I am afraid that he has great difficulty in relating to children that are his own age." Bryan's parents are also concerned about their child's ability to adjust in such a large school.

Academic Background

Bryan's teachers all agree that Bryan is extremely quiet and withdrawn in the classroom. Bryan does not interact with his peers. During the lunch hour Bryan always sits by himself. In his math class Mr. Roberts, the math teacher, has noted that Bryan is very reluctant to work math problems on the board at the front of the classroom. Mr. Roberts stated, "I believe that Bryan becomes very embarrassed when his peers notice his limp." Bryan never participates in classroom discussions, although his school work excels in math, science, and reading. Bryan does have problems in the area of written expression. He cannot use commas or quotation marks correctly. He also has difficulty in forming possessives. Occasionally, Bryan will fail to use capital letters or end punctuation marks.

Rationale for Initiating Peer Tutoring

Since Bryan excels in most subject areas, his teacher believe that a brief period of remediation would be a very successful method for the elimination of Bryan's problems in the area of written expression. The teachers also feel that the tutoring sessions might help Bryan to interact with his own peers. Bryan's teachers have chosen a tutor who has been noted to be very sensitive to other people's feelings. The peer tutoring sessions have been scheduled for a three-week trial period. The sessions will be held three times each week. At the end of this session, a decision will be made as to the continuation of the peer tutoring sessions.

General Objectives

1 Bryan should develop skills in the area of written expression.
2 Bryan should interact with a peer.

Specific Objectives

1 Bryan should use the correct punctuation mark at the end of sentences.
2 Bryan should capitalize proper names.
3 Bryan should use commas between city and state, between day of month and year, and to separate parts of a series.

Suggested Activities

1 The tutor reads a sentence and Bryan decides what punctuation mark should be placed at the end of the sentence.
2 Bryan finds two examples in his reading book of each type of punctuation mark that can be used at the end of a sentence.
3 The tutor gives Bryan a list of word categories that is composed of proper nouns. Bryan gives two examples for each category. Example: names of states — Texas, Iowa; months — January, March; names of shows — Benji, Star Trek.

4 The tutor copies one paragraph from Byan's history book and lets Bryan supply all necessary capital letters and end punctuation marks.

5 The tutor reviews the uses of the comma and lets Bryan list them on a sheet of paper. Bryan then places the necessary commas on a worksheet and tells the tutor why a comma is necessary.

6 Bryan finds ten examples of commas used in sentences in the newspaper.

Materials

1 Reading book
2 History book
3 Worksheets
4 Newspaper

Evaluation

The evaluation will be conducted at the end of the three-week peer tutoring sessions.

1 Given 10 sentences, Bryan should place all necessary capital letters and end punctuation marks with 100 percent accuracy.

2 Given 10 sentences, Bryan should place all necessary commas with 100 percent accuracy.

3 Given a paragraph, Bryan should place all necessary capital letters, commas, and end punctuation marks with 90 percent accuracy.

Tutor's Comments

Tutee:	Marsha
Grade:	Sophomore in High School
Subject:	Reading
Tutor:	Linda

TUTEE'S CASE DESCRIPTION

Family Background

Marsha is currently a sophomore in high school. Marsha lives with her parents and an older sister who is a senior in high school. At the present time Marsha is not getting along very well with either her parents or her sister. Marsha is very talkative while her sister is rather quiet. Marsha's sister has always made higher grades than Marsha. Marsha recently told her parents that "she didn't want to stay home and study all the time" and that "she certainly did not want to be like her sister." Marsha's parents complain that she stays out beyond her curfew time and that they suspect she is meeting boys after leaving the house; they think that Marsha should not be dating until next summer. Since the beginning of her sophomore year, Marsha states that her parents do not treat her fairly.

Academic Background

Marsha is very outgoing and enthusiastic about extra-curricular school activities. Marsha relates very well with her peers and has numerous friends. Marsha is not very interested in academic subjects. Frequently she fails to complete her homework assignments on time. Marsha is often tardy to classes. Until this year Marsha has been a C student but unless her study habits improve, her grades will be lower during this semester. Marsha's teachers describe her as being a very capable student but completely unmotivated. Marsha's strengths lie in the areas of math, art, drama, and home economics. She is averaging below a C in English and biology at the present time. Her English teacher, Mrs. Martin, and biology teacher, Mr. Sparks, agree that Marsha needs further direction in writing paragraphs since this is a basic unit of any written report. Since Marsha is experiencing problems in interacting with authority figures, the teachers have decided that she would accomplish more by working with someone her own age. Marsha will be assigned a tutor who is now a junior. The peer tutoring session will be initially scheduled for two weeks. During this two-week period, Marsha and her tutor will work daily for forty-five minutes. The results of this session will determine if peer tutoring should be continued.

General Objectives

1 Marsha should improve the quality of her reading comprehension.
2 Marsha should develop the ability to express herself through the usage of written language.

Specific Objectives

1 After listening to a paragraph, Marsha should express the main idea of the paragraph.
2 Marsha should be able to find the topic sentence of a paragraph.
3 Marsha should write a paragraph that contains a topic sentence and maintains the subject of the paragraph.

Suggested Activities

1 The tutor reads a paragraph from Marsha's biology book, and Marsha states the main idea of the paragraph.
2 Marsha reads aloud and discusses paragraphs from her biology book with her tutor. Marsha underlines the topic sentence of each paragraph.
3 Marsha reads a series of paragraphs on a worksheet and marks out any sentences that do not fall under the main thought of the paragraph.
4 The tutor gives Marsha a subject such as Disco Dancing and Marsha constructs three topic sentences that could be used to discuss the subject. Marsha writes a paragraph for each topic sentence.

Materials

1 Marsha's biology book
2 Worksheets

EVALUATION

The evaluation will be obtained at the close of the three-week session of peer tutoring.

1 Given a paragraph, Marsha should underline the topic sentence.
2 Given a paragraph, Marsha should delete any sentences that do not follow the main idea of the paragraph.
3 Marsha should compose a paragraph that contains a topic sentence and at least three other sentences.

Tutor's Comments

6
ORGANIZATION FOR LARGE-SCALE PEER TUTORING IN THE SCHOOLS

In this book, the authors have discussed in some detail the mechanics of developing and implementing peer tutoring programs in classrooms and other educational situations. It is our intent to provide a detailed guide to be used in the development and implementation of peer tutoring programs. In this chapter we shall discuss the elements that contribute to the potential for success of large-scale tutorial programs. We shall also discuss the strategies by which interested educators can present to school administrators, in a convincing manner, the advantages of tutorial programs. Of interest in this area will be the potential effects of a system-wide and school-wide tutorial program. We shall present examples of successful large-scale projects as documentation of tutoring's positive outcomes. We shall also examine the advantages of a systematic assessment of the outcomes of peer tutoring when it is employed over many classrooms. As an aid to implementation, we have appended checklists for use in setting up actual tutorial programs.

While the factors that influence a small-scale tutorial program are by no means few in number, large-scale programs appear to involve an even greater complex of elements that will affect outcomes. For example, the mechanics of setting up a small tutorial program in one classroom include choosing students to be tutored and students to tutor, and the development of a schedule under which students can meet in tutorial pairs. It is apparent that the more classrooms and children involved in a tutorial program, the more complicated will become the processes of selecting and pairing students, as well as creating a schedule which will be satisfactory to participating students and teachers. Another instance of the greater complexity of large-scale programs is in the assessment of progress made by students during their tutorial sessions. A teacher in one classroom can take time to assess quickly and accurately the progress of all students involved in a tutorial program. When several classroom groups of students are involved, a schedule for followup testing will become necessary. More structured and formalized methods of assessing student progress become necessary to provide each teacher with detailed information regarding the success or failure of their students.

To illustrate this point further, we shall cite several examples of small-scale programs that grew into system-wide programs. While the reasons for more extensive adaptation of a tutorial program will vary, one fact is manifest: the early efforts at peer tutoring met with success for students who were experiencing difficulties in the regular classroom. Children were learning and communicating with each other, in some instances for the first time. The local school administrators touted the success of the programs to other administrators and established a belief that peer tutoring could work in other settings.

Transfer of programs from one setting to another is not a one-step process. Every setting has its own unique blend of people. The building principal who supports a program in peer tutoring is an important element to the success of any program. Just as important is the attitude of teachers in the schools. Initiating any tutorial program requires work and much attention to how the program is to be organized. The manner in which teachers work and communicate together will affect how tutorial programs are ultimately developed and implemented. The students presently in the school influence the directions in which tutorial programs develop.

The factors that contribute to the success or failure of one local program or a series of independent local programs may, on the other hand, have little or no effect on other programs set up in a school system. The individuals who work to develop a system-wide program must be aware of the several keys to setting up any tutorial program (see Table 5.1), as well as the relative importance of these factors at different points in the program.

TABLE 5.1. Checklist for Organizing a Peer Tutorial Program

Important Factors	Accomplished	Not Accomplished
1 School staff identifies a need for change in working with students.		
2 School staff determines that peer tutoring will meet the needs of students and school staff.		
3 Principal and/or other administrative staff are involved in development of program.		
4 Tutorial project staff is specified; coordinator(s) of program is determined.		
5 Determination is made of needs for materials, space, and time.		
6 Project staff develops goals for tutorial program.		
7 Process is specified for (a) developing materials; (b) organizing session lessons; (c) locating space for sessions; (d) scheduling sessions; organization of efforts of all tutorial staff.		
8 The means of assessing program outcomes is determined, with staff assigned to this program component.		
9 Other pretutorial decisions are made—methods of selecting tutors and learners, method of pairing and training.		
10 When appropriate, pretutorial tests on content areas are given to children being tutored.		
11 Process is specified for communicating program results with central administrative staff.		
12 Project staff develops a plan for sequence of tutorial activities.		

For example, one consideration in developing a large-scale program is the *structure* that will encompass the overall program. Included in this consideration will be such elements as goals for the total program and organization of participating schools in the local program. If goals and organization considerations are haphazardly developed, the chances for the success of the total program will most certainly be in jeopardy. Individual factors present in large-scale programs often must be considered in a definite sequence. For example, Table 5.2 details a series of steps in the implementation of a system-wide tutorial program. Administrators of a tutorial project using this

TABLE 5.2.   Checklist for System-Wide Tutoring

	Factor	*Accomplished*	*Not Accomplished*
1	Need for system-wide tutorial program is established.		
2	Responsibility for developing the concept is assigned.		
3	Organization of coordinating unit for tutorial program is established.		
4	System for monitoring functioning of central unit is established.		
5	Mechanism for communicating with participating schools is established.		
6	Central unit sets goals for system-wide tutorial program.		
7	Participating schools set local goals for tutorial program.		
8	Training program is developed by central unit for system-wide use.		
9	Network for system-wide dissemination of tutorial strategies and materials is developed.		
10	Tutorial program is implemented as individual schools receive format for tutorial sessions.		
11	Central unit provides feedback to local schools on progress towards goals.		

checklist will discover that program achievements will build on each other. A direction in the program will be set early in the staff's efforts and can continue in this manner, given that the staff is comfortable with the program. Setting up a tutorial program in a less organized fashion undoubtedly will lengthen the time for implementation of the program and thus increase the workload on the tutorial staff.

As noted, the large-scale tutorial program does involve a more complex organization of efforts than does a small-scale program. Participating teachers, administrators, and students must be assigned tasks on an established schedule. Efforts of all participants must be and remain in harmony, combining to achieve program goals. The authors emphasize here and throughout this book the importance of establishing and maintaining a definite structure to the program, including procedures related to the activities of participants, the content of the sessions, and the assessment procedures utilized.

RATIONALE FOR LARGE-SCALE TUTORIAL PROGRAMS

Some differences between small- and large-scale tutorial programs have been discussed. This section will present some reasons for the implementation of large-scale tutorial programs in a school system. The most obvious reason is that programs can work in producing learning gains for students, *and* with a work force that frees teachers for other activities. An important consideration prior to system-wide adoption of a tutorial program is that the efforts of teachers at one school will influence the efforts of teachers at other schools. For example, many tutorial programs have focused on the development of materials to be used exclusively in tutoring sessions. Tutorial materials developed for a reading content area in one school could be used in other schools. In a program established in West Texas, a central administrative office gathered materials used across the schools in a system-wide program and shared these materials with other schools requesting materials on a particular subject. A decision by a school system to implement tutoring across a number of settings will necessitate, in most instances, the creation of a central organizing force to coordinate the dissemination of tutorial techniques and materials throughout the system.

The administrator reading this section will be considering the increase in teacher workload that would result from a system-wide program. A benefit of a central coordinating unit is that the workload on individual teachers and individual schools will be lessened as materials and strategies developed in the system are shared by participating schools. The trade-off in utilizing central administrative staff instead of independently-working local programs will favor the central unit. Not only will teacher workload decrease, but the cost of materials (both development and replication) will diminish. Materials can be assessed for applicability system-wide, with low-cost, large-scale means of reproduction being applied to materials that have use in many settings.

While a central unit offers advantages in the organization of a system-wide tutorial program, participants in local school programs can be utilized in the training of new program staff in other locations. All teachers working in the system on a tutorial project can be considered to form a nucleus of resource people, available to help team members in the fine points of implementing a tutorial program. In-service training of the team can be accomplished at one time, lessening the investment of time and resources in a more scattered method of training staff. Some system-wide programs have communicated their successful methods across the system using a newsletter format. Other low-cost means of disseminating results can accomplish the same purpose.

One important consideration in the implementation of a system-wide tutorial program is that seed monies for large-scale projects are often available from state and federal funding sources. Such funds can be actively pursued to lessen a local district's initial investment in a tutorial program.

PEER TUTORING AT THE SYSTEM-WIDE LEVEL

Many of the more recent studies of peer tutorial programs (as detailed in Chapter 2) have been on programs in large cities, in which school administrators have been seeking a solution to the low achievement evidenced by students living in these locations. (This is not to suggest, of course, that large cities imply low academic achievement; in fact, low academic achievement is affected by a large number of factors that occur in school districts of varying

sizes.) In many of the school systems adopting large-scale peer tutorial programs, the tutoring was a means to a variety of ends. These included both increasing the skills of the children being tutored, and in
providing the tutors with paid employment. In most school districts,
staffs of tutorial programs have experienced little difficulty in
locating volunteers for the position of paid tutor. From the successes
and failures of these earlier efforts have come clues as to how to
structure and implement a peer tutorial program at a system-wide
level. Before going into the specific determinants of a tutorial program, let's look at two examples of such programs.

A Large City, System-wide Program

In the early 1970s, teachers of special education classes in a Southwestern city were concerned with the needs of the bilingual children
in their classrooms. To help these children develop greater language
competencies, the teachers paired their students daily for brief experiences in talking to each other. In the peer tutoring program,
Mexican-American, black, and Anglo students participated from the
classrooms of the concerned teachers. Not content to merely talk to
each other, several pairs of students asked to be allowed to work
with each other on a more extended basis. Seizing on this opportunity, the teachers began to provide the students with materials to
complete during their daily sessions. The teachers reported their
success in assisting their students in working with each other during
a staff meeting at their school. Present at this meeting were the
principal, special education and psychological consultants, the
speech therapist, and other supportive personnel. All participants
at the meeting recognized the potential for helping students by
utilizing peer tutoring methods.

Later in the school year, with the assistance of the principal in
providing materials for tutorial activities and time for teachers
to develop materials for the daily sessions, three-fourths of the
school's faculty participated in a cross-grade tutorial program.
Students from regular *and* special education classes worked at
learning activities (including reading, spelling, and math) within
a tutorial arrangement. Pupils from the higher grades were paired
with younger students in the school. Two teachers shared the

responsibility for coordinating space and time arrangements for daily sessions. A volunteer committee of teachers cooperated in determining the content of the tutorial materials. A division of labor resulted, with different teachers taking responsibility for developing the lessons in reading, spelling, and math. Several teachers in the upper grades received extensive assistance from their students in preparing materials.

The principal of the school was pleased with the tutorial program for several reasons. Initially, the program appeared to spring from the efforts of a few teachers who were convinced of the potential for success using tutorial arrangements. The conviction of these teachers made it appear that the program could work in many classrooms with little added responsibility for the principal. (As a possible hidden motive, the principal saw the potential for increasing the academic performance of his bilingual students, children who had previously experienced little success in his school. As many educators readily recognize, the performance of students in a school has a definite effect on how a principal of that school is perceived by his or her superiors.)

When the support team and other teachers in the school became interested in applying tutoring strategies in more classrooms, the principal talked with the teachers who had first used such a program. The principal was made aware of the needs for space, time, and additional materials to create a viable school-wide tutorial program. This principal contributed a great deal to the eventual success of the program. He encouraged teachers to develop their own materials and programs. He provided the opportunity for teachers to meet to discuss the "how to's" of developing, implementing, and monitoring a cross-grade tutorial program. As the school year progressed, the principal secured funds for the purchase of additional materials for the tutorial program.

The key to the spread of peer tutorial programs from this one school throughout the entire school system resulted from two interacting events. First, the principal, exhibiting justifiable pride, mentioned the success of the then-innovative program to as many fellow principals as possible in their monthly administrative meetings. Then an assistant superintendent was informed of the program and its results and encouraged the principal to solicit the assistance of the district's administrative staff in evaluating the program. This conversation led to members of the system's research department doing an official pilot program at the school. The goal of this effort was to determine the degree to which the tutoring activities was helping the students.

Findings were sufficiently positive for the administrative staff to apply for state funding from the State Education Agency to implement a tutorial program that would be designed primarily for bilingual and other students experiencing difficulties in English language development. Grant monies were approved and tutorial activities begun in ten elementary schools. In a snow-balling fashion, the success of the majority of programs using the tutorial strategy led to more local monies being made available for the creation of new tutorial programs. Teachers from the initial tutorial programs spread the word in meetings during in-service time with fellow professionals. Project directors trained volunteers from any district school that wished to develop and implement a tutorial program. Today, almost every school in the system uses some form of tutorial activities with its students. Funds for the activities are now derived from local campus budgets. Administrators, teachers, students, and their parents have been very pleased with the results: greater student achievement and satisfaction with learning.

A Small City, System-wide Project

A consultant to a small Midwestern school system was invited to examine the classroom climate of the city's largest junior high school. During the preceding two years, the school's principal and superintendent had become disturbed about the lack of interest of the students for learning activities. With this lack of interest came both increased classroom disruptions and decreased academic performance from the majority of students in the school. The school's instructional staff had tried everything from getting tough with disruptive students to implementing a reward system for increased performance on tests administered in various classes. While each remedy had a short-term effect, the underlying problems appeared no closer to solution.

The consultant who visited the school to examine the situation was already familiar with both the characteristics of the student body and the general approaches to learning used by the teachers. The consultant, based on her previous perceptions of the school, believed that the seemingly recent appearance of unmotivated and disruptive students had its basis in the attitudes of teachers and administrators towards the learning process *in toto*. The educational process, as seen by these individuals, was a straightforward proposition—teachers were to teach and students to learn. The goal of learning, for the most part, was for the students to memorize materials that would be tested through periodic examinations. This system of teaching had seemed to work in the past and was expected to be equally effective in the present and future.

As the reader is well aware, changing attitudes towards teaching or any other topic is a difficult matter at best. In a weekly session with the superintendent and the principal, the consultant communicated general perceptions of the school's situation. The superintendent confirmed many of the consultant's perceptions. The principal mentioned his concern that meaningful involvement between teachers and students was low. The three professionals agreed that memorization, as a basic teaching strategy, should be only part of the learning process. Obviously, memorization should seldom, if ever, be used as an end in itself. A number of suggestions for change were generated at the meeting. These ideas centered on increasing the involvement level of students in the classroom, making the learning process more enjoyable, and giving students a greater feeling of responsibility for the learning that was occurring in their classrooms.

The principal and the consultant discussed these perceptions with the teaching and support staff at the junior high school. The principal was somewhat surprised to find that the majority of his teachers shared concerns about the level of learning of students. Many teachers, again to the principal's surprise, strongly agreed that memorization had a limited place in teaching students various curricular tasks. The consensus among the staff was that some change must be initiated. Taking the path of least resistance, the teachers and support personnel supported the principal's recommendation that the consultant continue to work with the school to develop activities that would increase involvement, help students to think critically, and motivate the students to perform more effectively in the classroom.

The consultant recognized the almost classic elements of a problem that could be lessened with application of the educational strategies developed by William Glasser, among others. This approach, referred to as Reality Therapy, is directed at the concerns voiced by school staff. While the actual implementation of Reality Therapy principles in the school is not of direct relevance to this writing, the inclusion of peer tutoring activities as a means to get students involved in the teaching-learning process is. Both cross- and same-grade tutoring activities were initiated. Many students were able to experience both tutor and tutee roles. With tutoring activities came greater interest by the students in what they were learning and how they were being taught.

The superintendent saw the increase in student interest as a reflection of peer tutoring's potential to make students more aware of the learning process and its demands on the teacher and learner. With his support, the consultant worked with other city schools that were experiencing the after-effects of low student motivation and achievement. Principals and teachers received information in their training programs on implementation procedures for peer tutoring in the classroom. Because of limited financial assets, the school system did not provide additional staff or materials to schools that were developing tutorial programs.

ELEMENTS OF A SUCCESSFUL
SYSTEM-WIDE PROGRAM

The two examples of actual peer tutoring programs in a large and small school system demonstrate that system-wide programs in peer tutoring seem to follow the success of smaller scale projects in the school system. Successful system-wide tutorial programs often evolve from much smaller programs in individual schools. Close examination of the examples reveals several common elements that contributed to eventual system-wide adoption and subsequent success. These factors include:

1 The staff of the pilot tutoring project was open to assistance in project implementation and evaluation from a variety of outside resource people.
2 The pilot project had the strong backing of the principal and administrative staff.

3 The success of pilot efforts contributed to the spread of project activities to other schools.

4 Administrators provided encouragement and, in the first example, financial assistance to school staff to use in developing materials.

In both examples, the principals freed interested staff members from some of their regular duties so that they could receive training on the tutorial process, and later could concentrate on implementing tutorial strategies. Let's examine these elements more closely.

The staff in each of the two schools described above was faced with an uncomfortable situation that is frequently encountered by many educators. Many students were performing at less than their potential in the classroom. Rather than ignore the situation or wait until it changed for the better (when it could just as easily have changed for the worse), the staff members examined their particular circumstances, continually seeking the roots of their scholastic difficulties. In the first example, bilingual children were having trouble acquiring English language skills. Teachers noticed that bilingual children seldom worked with children who were not bilingual. In the peer tutoring program, the bilingual children could model their language behaviors after those of the other children in the class. The teacher noticed an added benefit. The daily sessions promoted interaction among all of the students, and led to greater mingling of children both in and out of the classroom. When the school district in the first example adopted peer tutoring programs system-wide, similar effects were noted by teachers and researchers in several schools.

In the second illustration, the teachers and administrative staff were well aware of the symptoms of student malaise. The school staff was uncomfortable with the situation and was searching for methods to increase student involvement. The services of an outside consultant helped to focus attention on methods to increase involvement of students and to challenge them to accept greater responsibility for their learning. Methods such as peer tutoring met the needs of the local campus situation, and eventually were practiced in other schools throughout the city.

The next factor in the successful system-wide adoption of peer tutoring was the strong support of the school's principals and administrative staffs. The principals encouraged the initial efforts of the teachers who implemented peer tutoring in their classrooms. As the reader is well aware, the teacher who does not receive the encouragement and other *visible* support of the principal has to work twice as hard to make an innovative program successful. The principal plays a key role in the eventual success of a peer tutoring program. This professional is responsible for or directly involved in all aspects of the academic program of the school. While in reality few principals have the time to devote an extensive portion of their day to the school's academic program, the principal's support of teacher-initiated activities affects the tone of that school's learning program. In the examples, the principals provided much more than encouragement to their teachers. For example, they provided blocks of time to be used by teachers in exploring peer tutorial options. Later, flexible class assignments were arranged so that teacher time could be devoted to maintenance and monitoring of the tutorial program. As an additional means of support, the principals contributed materials to be used in the tutorial activities.

As these examples illustrate, another key role of the principal was in communicating to other principals and administrators regarding the success of the tutoring efforts in his school. By spreading the word the principal in the first example was informed about potential funding for a tutoring project in his school. Central office staff, impressed with the program, asked their evaluation team to examine the program for use in other schools. This soon occurred as schools across the city developed and implemented their own tutorial programs.

The success of the initial projects was a basic factor in the support of central office administrators for the implementation of peer tutoring programs in additional schools. One element that every school administrator notices is the program that *helps children.* Of similar importance is the factor of the cost effectiveness of tutoring activities. The programs discussed in the examples required few additional monies to start and maintain tutoring activities. In both instances, the redirection of existing funds provided the majority of monies to be used in tutoring activities.

With the validity of the pilot projects demonstrated, members of the central administrative staff were more open to alloting additional monies and materials for the programs. In the second example, the system's superintendent was involved in helping the school staff from the start to discover a new approach to increasing student involvement and academic output. An assistant superintendent in the first example was important to the eventual spread of tutorial programs in his district when he encouraged additional funding for the program through state agencies.

As a general rule, the involvement of the principal and administrators from the school system will promote the likelihood of success of early efforts at starting a tutorial program. Additionally, as administrators become aware of the program, they are more likely to offer the support of their staff in assisting program efforts. This is especially important both in the replication of tutorial programs in other schools and in the careful documentation of tutoring activities. By consistently monitoring ongoing activities, administrators are able to assess the likelihood of acquiring nonschool district funds for the extended development of tutorial programs.

The advantages of the peer tutoring programs in the first school thus were experienced at other schools in the system, one outcome of school administrators being impressed by the benefits and cost-effectiveness of tutorial programs. Benefits of the program included more frequent interactions among children of different ethnic groups, increased rates of acquisition of English language skills by bilingual children, greater involvement in the learning process, and greater acceptance of responsibility by students for the development and implementation of academic activities.

Peer Tutoring at the Campus Level

While the previous examples of system-wide programs necessarily began with programs that originated on one school campus, it will be instructive to examine tutorial programs at single campuses that were not successfully replicated in other schools. We will examine these examples closely for the factors that contributed to this outcome.

A residental program for emotionally disturbed children was developed in one city to meet the very special academic and affective needs of this district's student population. Staff members were trained primarily to work with emotionally disturbed children. Support from additional departments of the school system was ongoing, so that materials were not lacking for any phase of the program. Program activities were identified as being "very special", that is, designed specifically for the target population. One staff member, Mrs. Hollis, proposed at a staff meeting that peer tutorial activities could be of some help in allowing students to work together on a common task. Previously, students worked on an individual or small-group basis with the teacher. Mrs. Hollis was concerned with the difficulty exhibited by several students in attempts to communicate verbally with other students. Many of these students were nonverbal the majority of the time, both in school and in the dormitory. Tutoring activities offered a relatively low-risk means for students to work together in the classroom. Peer tutoring was attempted with a select number of students on a trial basis. Results of the program were encouraging. Participating students enjoyed the activities, were able to successfully complete the brief daily sessions, and, to the delight of the staff, became more verbal with peers following involvement in the program. Not every student was able to participate in these activities, however. A few students were not able to accept the responsibilities involved in either the tutor or learner roles. These students had either become withdrawn when introduced to a tutorial partner or had exhibited emotional and behavioral outbursts during the sessions.

Teacher participants in the program presented their strategy for increasing student involvement in academic activities during their monthly meetings with staff members from other special education programs. While teachers in these programs had used some version of peer tutoring in their classrooms, there was not an organized approach to implementing tutorial activities with more than one or two other teachers. The special education teachers had infrequent contact with their regular education peers in schools throughout the city. Few of the teachers communicated their successful teaching strategies to their colleagues. Indeed, most regular education teachers in the system saw few similarities between teaching methods used with children in their classrooms and those used in special education classrooms. The label "special" applied to the educational activities in a classroom carried the connotation "different" and, thus, not readily applicable. The residential treatment program was considered to be even more "special" in that educational and psychological services were provided over a twenty-four hour period. More discussion of this program will follow the next example.

In a small Southern school system, Miss Epperson, a new teacher in a reading class, commonly read professional journals in her field. She noticed occasional references in periodicals to the success of peer tutoring programs that focused on the acquisition of reading skills. Being conscious of her status as the newest member of the teaching staff in her school, Miss Epperson was dedicated to providing her children with the best possible program in reading. Peer tutoring was to be part of her total program. Starting from scratch, the teacher located materials that could be used in daily tutoring sessions. She designated one corner of her room as a quiet spot in which tutorial pairs could work. She discussed her plans with another young teacher, who also taught reading. Together, the two shared students who participated in the activities.

The tutorial students enjoyed the opportunity to visit another class to see their friends. Learning was occurring during the sessions and teachers were pleased until more and more students wanted to become involved in the program. Both teachers began to feel swamped with the responsibility of developing lessons, scheduling time for the sessions, pairing the students, and finally being sure that the students were staying on task during their sessions. Rather than ask their principal or other teachers for advice, the teachers permitted the tutoring program to become gradually more restricted. They did this by allowing fewer and fewer students to participate in the activities. Eventually, students lost interest as the teachers implemented other larger group (non-peer tutoring) activities in the classroom.

The teachers in the last example failed to capitalize on the common threads of instructional strategy found in all classrooms. Every teacher would like to provide his or her students with the best possible instructional program, one that meets the students' affective and cognitive needs. But by creating boundaries around the activities in any one classroom, the teacher decreases the flow of ideas and strategies on teaching to colleagues. The first example highlights the frequent lack of sharing of ideas between special and regular classroom teachers. The second example illustrates the consequences of a new teacher's hesitancy to ask for aid from more experienced teachers when faced with a problem in her classroom.

As a result of such communication deficits, the success of individual peer tutoring programs had little chance to spread outside of the classroom. In the second example, no mention of peer tutoring activities even leaked from the two teachers' classrooms. In neither example was the principal nor other administrative staff of the school system provided with information on the special activities. No attempt was made to document tutorial strategies, or to evaluate in a structured manner the outcomes of peer tutorials. Without such efforts, there would be little opportunity to justify additional funding for tutorial projects. A more detailed explanation on the advantages of a strategy to assess tutorial outcomes appears in a section later in this chapter.

The four examples mentioned thus far provide no information on the training of tutors to fulfill the responsibilities of their position. Many successful tutoring programs contain a training component. While details on the training of tutors will not be listed here, it is important to include the time and materials needed to train tutors in considerations prior to the implementation of a tutorial program. Training costs are less of a problem than the time needed to complete training activities. Time for training tutors is an important issue in introducing peer tutoring at both the campus and the system level. Training programs will become less of a burden on teacher time as more teachers become involved in a school. In some districts that use peer tutoring in several schools, training activities are offered at central locations for clusters of schools, thus cutting down further on time required to train groups of tutors. Other considerations that could be applied to "go/no go" decisions on the development of tutorial programs may come to the minds of the readers. These considerations, as they reflect the characteristics of local schools and individual districts, should be included in discussions with teachers, principals, support staff, and administrators who are working on the organization of the tutorial program.

Organization to Evaluate Tutoring Outcomes

Throughout this chapter, and for the remainder of this book, frequent mention will be made of the importance of systematically evaluating the outcomes of a peer tutorial program. By itself, assessment of outcomes is important to project staff. In addition, regular assessment of outcomes provides the ammunition to administrators who may wish to seek additional materials and monies for tutorial activities. Any proposal to an outside-of-district agency to acquire additional funds will need to include a detailed enumeration of the efforts that will be taken to assess expected outcomes. With an evaluation strategy already in operation, a school will have collected data which will help shape hypotheses and strategies to incorporate into funding proposals.

A well-structured assessment component in a tutorial program is good politics. With data on the specifics of a tutorial program, project staff will be providing school administrators with the facts that will communicate to school patrons and board members the viability of the tutorial approach. One outcome of this flow of hard data to these groups is that local funds could be designated for tutorial activities. Giving exposure of the program at this level increases the chances of the program being replicated at other locations in the system.

The assessment of the outcomes of peer tutoring, whether these outcomes reflect cognitive or affective gains by students, provides important information to program staff. The outcomes on which tutorial staff focus will reflect the goals for the particular tutorial program. For example, in one program the goal of the tutorial project staff was to improve reading ability levels one month for every two weeks spent by a child in tutoring activities. The project staff employed a locally developed test of reading ability level to compare scores of students on a biweekly assessment of reading levels. Goals for a tutorial program are best specified in readily obtainable and observable behavioral terms. In such a format, the task of assessing the accomplishment of that goal is a relatively straightforward task.

When goals for the tutorial program reflect process factors or affective variables, the assessment strategy is simplified again if the individual objectives can be specified in behavioral terms.

7
PEER TUTORING AND THE HANDICAPPED STUDENT

In the previous chapters, the authors have attempted to present the reader with the major elements involved in establishing a peer tutoring program in a school environment. These procedures, if followed, should provide the teacher with a viable means of establishing and maintaining tutorial programs either within the confines of the regular classroom or within the context of an entire school. It should be apparent to most educators, however, that when the tutorial effort is expanded to include children who have been labeled "exceptional" or "handicapped," certain additional considerations will frequently need to be made in order to provide for those students' unique instructional needs. The purpose of this chapter is to acquaint the reader with (1) the exceptional students and their problems, (2) programs that have proven effective with the exceptional student, and (3) recommendations for program modifications when planning peer tutoring activities for the exceptional student.

EDUCATIONAL PROGRAMS FOR THE HANDICAPPED

From an historial standpoint, the education of handicapped children has abounded with much controversy and debate. The primary source of contention regarding the education of handicapped students has centered around the question of what type of instructional setting will best meet their academic and affective needs. During the past fifty years in American schools, the main vehicle for educating the child with special needs has been to segregate them into "special" classrooms that, presumably, were designed to provide opportunities geared to the child's unique educational needs. The rationale underlying the relatively isolated educational placement was that these students were so "deviant" in most facets of learning that they required the full-time attention of specially trained teachers. In addition, it was frequently believed that these pupils, if allowed to interact extensively with "normal" students, would provide negative influence, although there was no evidence that this was, in fact, often the case. Parent groups were adamant in their insistence that children who had been labeled handicapped be maintained in special classrooms so that other children would not need to come into contact with them.

While there can be little question that the self-contained classroom for certain handicapped children is indeed justified, it is obviously inappropriate for those handicapped students who exhibit only mild to moderate academic and/or behavioral problems. For example, trainably mentally retarded students generally require the services of a special teacher on a full-time basis in order that they be provided appropriate educational opportunities. These children, in all likelihood, will need some type of supervision throughout their lives and should not be expected to learn at a rate that is commensurate with that of normal children. Students who demonstrate severe emotional problems and/or are threats to both themselves and to others, need to be maintained in environments where their destructive and harmful tendencies can be effectively ameliorated. On the other hand, students who have been labeled as learning disabled, educably mentally retarded, or educationally handicapped, exhibit classic behavior similar to their normal peers in most regards, with the exception of academic under-achievement. In most schools the current trend is to educate these students within the confines of the regular classroom to the maximum extent possible. This process, frequently termed *mainstreaming*, enables these students to receive the attention of both the regular teacher and the special education teacher. An additional benefit of this administrative process is that the mildly handicapped student receives the opportunity to interact with peers who evidence little or no academic and/or social difficulties.

It will come as little surprise to most experienced teachers that, while there are many positive benefits to be gained for the mildly handicapped child being placed in a regular classroom, this practice does have the potential to create some problems. The major problem to be faced by the regular teacher is from the standpoint of how to provide needed individual instruction to mildly handicapped pupils without neglecting other students in the classroom. It is within this framework that peer tutoring can become a highly viable source of aid to the teacher. The utilization of other students to program and present materials or assist in instruction to handicapped students can be an equitable means of providing needed instructional assistance to those students.

Not only may handicapped students function as recipients of a peer tutoring effort, they also may be effectively utilized as tutors with younger children. The opportunity for these students to function in the role of the tutor has demonstrated positive effects regarding the acceptance of responsibility (i.e., self-concept) as well as review of material that is traditionally presented at lower grade levels. While the literature in this area of peer tutoring has not been extensive, there are a number of programs that have been proven successful when employing tutors who have been labeled as handicapped. The following section will outline the major components of these programs and will be followed by a discussion of modifications that will need to be made when working with handicapped students of varying age levels.

EXISTING PROGRAMS FOR HANDICAPPED STUDENTS

In their book Gartner, Kohler and Riessman (1971) have discussed many studies that designed peer tutoring programs for "special" children. For example, in California, fifth- and sixth-grade teachers referred "problem children" to a peer tutoring project. "Problem children" were defined as those who exhibited discipline or other behavior problems in the classroom. The tutors worked with students who were on a pre-primary level. Tutoring areas were set aside in the pre-primary classroom and tutors were recruited to work with one or more pre-primary children at a time.

Other programs have been started for children who have been labeled as "slow learners" by teachers in their schools. A program in Missouri utilized the efforts of junior high school students who were deficient on basic elementary skills to work with elementary school students in the prescribed skills areas. The purpose of the program was to enable the tutors to re-learn the basic skills as well as to develop a more positive attitude regarding academic materials. A similar project in Nashville used a tutoring program to improve the self-concept of the tutors by involving them in teaching younger students. In addition to gains in self-concepts, the students became more proficient in content areas, improved in social skills, increased the analysis of various learning tasks, applied what they observed to their own learning styles, and improved attitudes toward school (Gartner, Kohler, and Riessman, 1971).

Many other programs have been developed that are in concert with the objectives of those programs discussed in the previous paragraph. Teachers and administrators have initiated programs that are intended to instill in the tutor a sense of pride in the accomplishments of their handicapped tutee. Working with this improved image of self, the tutor is more likely to apply himself/herself to academic tasks in the regular classroom. If the student tutor is a slow learner and has experienced a great deal of difficulty in adjusting to the demands of the classroom, the success of peer tutoring can be very beneficial. Because the role of a tutor is a demanding one, accomplishing these objectives frequently indicates to the student that he/she can complete a difficult task successfully. A student who who has been labeled handicapped is frequently in greater need than other students for confirmation of self-worth and academic competency. Therefore, many programs have recruited students from special education classrooms to work in peer tutoring programs. Galvin and Shoup have described a project in which special students helped others and themselves through peer tutoring experiences. Special students in this classroom were those who had been in the regular classroom and had begun withdrawing from both peers and teacher. These students had seemingly begun to "tune out" from the rest of the group. They were rarely completing their assignments and, consequently, were placed in special educational settings. Several of the students in these special classrooms were trained as pupil teachers. The purpose of the pupil teachers was to improve the reading levels of other students in the classroom. While the entire class was working on activities to improve reading, the pupil teachers were successful in helping the other students to increase their reading speed and reading achievement. Pupil teachers were especially benefited by the program; this fact is illustrated in that their total reading gains improved significantly. In a similar study in New York City, the staff of a medical center utilized first-grade children who were identified as requiring special education. These students were to be trained by sixth graders on general "readiness" activities. The sixth graders became experts at completing these tasks that were designed to overcome developmental problems of the first graders. Tutors assisted the project staff in evaluating the children and in training other tutors who came into the program. After a period of careful evaluation, the program was judged a success by the staff participants (Gartner, Kohler, and Riessman, 1971).

In another program that utilized children from regular classrooms to work with children with special learning needs, Evans and Potter (1974) described the training of sixth graders to tutor students with functional articulation disorders. Twenty-four six- to nine-year-olds were treated either by the tutors or by a speech clinician. Tutors were chosen both with and without histories of previous speech therapy. At the conclusion of the program, there was little difference in the articulatory proficiency of the tutees regardless of whether they worked with tutors or speech clinicians.

Collins and Calevro (1974) describe a peer tutoring program for special education students who are being mainstreamed through the use of a peer tutoring system and a modified academic curriculum. The objective of the peer tutoring activity was to improve the math skills of nine eighth graders. Students whose math skill deficiencies ranged from 3.8 to 6.6 years met daily with tutors for thirty minutes of instruction. After three months in the project, increases in math skills of the tutees varied from 4.8 months to 14.6 months per month of tutoring. The authors argued quite convincingly that the students benefited significantly by involvement in the peer tutoring program.

Several studies have described projects in which children labeled mentally retarded have benefited from peer tutoring while functioning both as tutors and tutees. Two reports of such projects are those of Engel (1974) and Harrington (1974). Engel describes a training program for upper-elementary-aged trainable retarded students. In this program, educably mentally retarded students served as tutors. These students, in addition to severe academic deficiencies, exhibited severe orthopedic or other disabling conditions that prevented them from participating in other public school programs. One period a day was established for the tutoring activities. The content of the sessions focused upon gross and fine motor activities. Some activities emphasized eye-hand coordination and other perceptual skills. Engel noted that involvement in the training of the students benefited both the tutee and the tutor. The trainable mentally retarded children seemed to enjoy the involvement with the other students and improved in general motor proficiency. Educable mentally retarded students who were serving as tutors developed greater self-confidence, communication skills, and feelings of self-worth. Harrington (1974) described a group of trainable mentally retarded students who were designated as "supervisors" of instructional tasks for classmates. The responsibilities given to these students fostered leadership abilities and confidence in the peer supervisor and helped to create a trust relationship between the two students. In an interesting modification of the typical peer tutoring procedure, any child who accomplished a task became eligible to assist other students and become a "supervisor" also. Since the abilities of the students varied widely, a pupil could be a tutor in several activities and yet receive tutoring in a wide number of other areas. Each student was able to promote his/her strengths and to receive help in activities in which he/she was weak. Harrington argued that in using this approach the teacher became the manager of the classroom and could devote greater time to observing the tutoring in the classroom and making recommendations for each child's academic program. Students in the classroom using this peer-supervisor method reported greater enjoyment with the learning process. Apparently, peer teaching with the trainable retarded students increased both independence and feeling of self-importance and self-worth for the children as well as those skills which were actually taught.

Wagner and Sternlicht (1975) instituted a very interesting project in which trainable mentally retarded adolescents in a residential school served as tutors for younger retarded children who were deficient in dressing and eating skills. The effects of the program on both the tutors and the learners in terms of acquiring and retaining self-maintenance skills and the social and personal adjustment of the parties were examined. Tutors received extensive training in dressing and eating techniques—a total of sixty hours was devoted to these training activities. The tutors were allotted time to teach the dressing and eating skills to their partners over periods of approximately twenty hours for each cluster of skills. The children were tutored in dressing skills for a period of sixteen days with fifty to seventy-five minutes per day devoted to these activities. Of special interest in this program was the training that was given to the tutors.

The training for the tutors included both pretutorial and in-service sessions. The content of the training program was based on the premise that the learners would best learn from a highly structured and sequential curriculum. The dressing and eating skills were ordered according to their level of difficulty. Before the tutoring was initiated, the children delineated as tutors were given both verbal instruction, staff demonstrations, and role-playing activities in which to sharpen their tutoring skills. During the tutoring phase, two staff members were present at all times during the activities between tutor and learner to provide feedback and support. Tutors were given as much opportunity as possible to function independent of staff members so that their interaction with learners could be spontaneous and yet in accord with project guidelines. The results of the study indicated that there was a significant improvement in dressing and eating skills for the students who received the tutoring from the adolescents in the project. The authors reported secondary gains; these included the increased ability for the learners to model behaviors of their tutors, as well as for the learners to attend more frequently to people and events in their environment. Inappropriate behaviors of the learners began to decrease. The authors report that incidents of restless behavior decreased as the students became more involved in the tutoring project; one student stopped pulling out her hair while another became less self-abusive while active in the program.

From Wagner and Sternlicht's observations of the handicapped adolescents serving as tutors, it was noted that a significant decrease was occurring in tutors' maladaptive behaviors. In the setting utilized in this project, with opportunities for a child to engage in interesting activities such as tutoring, there seemed to be less need for the tutors to demonstrate antisocial behavior. The authors also reported that tutors were more spontaneous in their expression of affection for others. Tutors increased in their ability to make responsible decisions and to rely less upon staff members for decision making. In addition, students became more involved in learning activities and less likely to become frustrated when working with others. The students began to pay more attention to their personal appearance. Some students began to modify their verbal behavior in more socially-accepted directions. The program used volunteers for the tutor position. Tutors retained their interest in the program throughout the duration of the project and reported their enjoyment of the activities. The results of this study indicated that a program which can train retarded students to teach other such students can have value for both the tutors and learners.

Brown, Fenrick, and Klemme (1971) have reported on a project in which trainable mentally retarded students have tutored other trainable mentally retarded students. The project was divided into five major parts. Continuance in the project was contingent upon completion of the content of each preceding part. The first portion of the program was designed to teach the trainable students approximations of the reading process. Using the prescribed procedures, students learned to orally read printed words in groups while working under conditions of individualized instruction. The students acquired information that was of functional value such as word labels and also learned relatively simple well-structured teaching procedures. In the initial part of the procedure, the tutors were provided with sets of words that they were to teach a peer. Two sets of words were involved. One group of words would be taught to one student and the second group of words taught to the other student. Students being trained at a later time would be requested to teach the groups of words to other students, so it was necessary for project staff to provide students with the experience of observing the teacher model group instructional procedures. A third group of words was compiled and taught to the students in a group instructional setting. Brown, Fenrick, and Klemme describe in some detail the specific teaching procedures used to train tutors.

The second part of the project was designed so that, using the teaching procedures utilized in the first segment, the students could teach others to read different words that they, in turn, had learned. The third segment of the project was designed to allow students to form teams of two members to help their classmates with the words they had mastered. The fourth segment of the project involved greater numbers of class members in the teaching program. The final portion of the project was designed to utilize these skills and the motivation demonstrated by the students to extend their reading program into a writing program for home-school communication. The authors of the project report that the project was an unqualified success. Not only did the students acquire the specific skills that were outlined for completion under each project segment, but they also used these skills to effectively teach other students. The implication of these studies is that a special education teacher may be able to arrange his/her classroom so that some of the students can assume responsibility for minor teaching activities and free the teacher for more intensive instructional programs. Brown et al. report that students seemed encouraged by their involvement in the project. Simply being included in a new and different activity proved exhilarating for these handicapped students. Armed with a sense of pride, the students reported their involvement to parents, siblings, and teachers.

The programs detailed above have indicated that children with special academic and affective needs can succeed in a tutoring program. The reader may have questions concerning the applicability of training and selection procedures, described in earlier chapters, to these special students. We will consider in the next section the several elements contingent upon the development of a peer tutoring program involving students with special learning needs. We also will discuss materials that can be used with these students. However, the authors believe that all students with motivation and minimum level of ability have something to contribute to teaching other students whether this be academic or social skills. Involvement in a peer tutoring program can lead to improved feelings of the children about themselves and their academic and social abilities. These students are better able to cope with pressures of the classroom environment.

IMPLEMENTING A PEER TUTORING PROGRAM
WITH SPECIAL STUDENTS

Several considerations must be made prior to implementing a peer tutoring program for children with special learning and affective needs. As with all tutoring programs, teachers involved in establishing the program will find it beneficial to attend to the following factors: (1) selection, (2) pairing, (3) training, (4) scheduling, (5) creating tutoring space, (6) materials, and (7) monitoring. When the population to be served by the project includes handicapped students, involved staff members may decide to emphasize the degree to which program procedures are specified prior to the beginning of tutoring. In many programs that have worked with special children, tutorial structure has been well specified before the initiation of the tutorial project. For example, in the study reported by Brown, Fenrick, and Klemme (1971), program structure was determined well before the start of the program so that the students could enter the tutorial session and receive a well-defined collection of content materials. The manner in which these materials were delivered to the students also was highly specified by project staff. In this particular instance, the student tutors were trainable mentally retarded children. Project staff hypothesized that the tutors would be better able to assume responsibility for the tutor role if they were given very explicit instructions on how to conduct tutoring activities. As a result, training was extensive, as was the followup on the tutor's activities upon implementing the program. Wagner and Sternlicht (1975) report another program in which trainable mentally retarded students worked with students with similar mental abilities. Again, training activities were very extensive and emphasized in great detail the nature of the tutoring activities.

Considerations in the selection of students to participate in tutoring may be quite simple. For example, a teacher of exceptional children served in a resource room (i.e., an educational setting designed for mildly handicapped students who spend a portion of each day in the regular classroom) may decide to implement a tutoring program with handicapped students. The students chosen as tutors for these students typically exhibit strengths in a particular tutorial content area. The tutees will be those students who are exhibiting below-level performance in that particular skill area. Pairing considerations are usually straightforward. Pupils may be matched on the basis of the degree to which they interact with each other in the classroom. More rigid selection and pairing standards may be developed by the individual teacher or project manager when these procedures are deemed necessary to the implementation of the project. However, if the goal of tutoring is to involve as many students as possible in the program, then all children should be given the opportunity to participate as tutor or learner. Scheduling of the tutorial pairs should be made explicit to the students involved in the project. If the students are to benefit from tutoring, a consistent and clearly specified time period in which to meet must be defined for the tutorial pairs. All students benefit from having a schedule to follow with their tutorial partner. Students with special learning and affective needs may benefit more than other students with this arrangement, in that the regular schedule is easy to learn and provides more certainty about the tutorial arrangement.

The teachers who implement a tutorial program with handicapped students may emphasize the comfort of the tutorial setting in which the students are meeting. When students have particular physical handicaps, the tutorial arrangements may be created so that these handicaps are minimized. For example, the space created for tutorial pairs to meet may be quite roomy and free from physical impediments when the students involved are in wheelchairs. Another instance in which a tutorial arrangement may be created to meet the comforts of the participants was observed by one of the authors. In this instance, the students who had no physical handicaps had negotiated with their teachers to conduct their tutoring while seated on a rug. The students were quite pleased with the arrangements. The teachers believed that the comfort of this arrangement helped the tutoring to proceed more smoothly.

Materials for students participating in a peer tutoring program are more likely to be of benefit to the tutors and tutees if these materials are both specific and relevant. This is true for all students who are engaged in a tutoring program. For students who have special learning and affective needs, the manner in which the materials are presented is even more important. The length of lessons may be shortened in tutorial programs for such students so that the children's physical and mental comfort are not unduly taxed. Lesson plans must be well structured and provide a great deal of feedback to the participants. Care should be taken that materials be presented in a manner in which staff members can readily observe tutorial activities in order to provide feedback to the tutor when the tutee's behavior or academic performance is not in accordance with the program guidelines. The importance of monitoring the tutorial process increases when the program is conducted with handicapped children. This holds true whether the special student is a tutor or tutee. The extent to which feedback is given to both tutor and learner can influence the performance of the individual children towards meeting their tutorial objectives. As in the case of other tutorial programs, the imagination and creativity of the teachers involved in the program will determine the extent to which the program meets its objectives. Teachers who are aware of the strengths and limitations of their special students will be better able than other teachers to develop and implement a tutorial program appropriate to their students' unique needs. The experienced teacher with knowledge in the learning and behavioral problems exhibited by children is probably the person most qualified to assist or direct in the development of a tutorial program. Regrettably, few tutorial programs that involved students with special learning and affective needs have been described in educational journals. The teacher who endeavors to develop such a program will have few models on which to pattern his/her program. However, given the suggestions in previous chapters, the teacher should be able to establish a program that will involve the participants in meaningful learning activities. Once the program is off the ground, modifications can be made in structure and content to better meet the program objectives and needs of handicapped students.

8
VARIATIONS OF THE PEER TUTORING MODEL

The preceding chapters in this book have focused on the elements that compose programs in peer tutoring. The authors have covered the specifics of setting up a peer tutoring program in the process considering the peer tutoring programs that typically exist in primary and secondary schools. Peer tutoring, in the strict use of the term, has been distinguished from cross-age tutoring, but in both instances, the participating students have been children. Techniques and strategies that were presented have been in the context of the typical school program experienced by most children. In this chapter, the authors will explore additional situations in which peer tutoring has been used as an arrangement for learning. The settings in which tutoring occurs influence the structure and methods employed by educators in the implementation of tutoring. A program in which adults work with status offender youth will be examined in detail, as well as other programs in which tutorial project managers thought it feasible to employ adult tutors. Additional consideration will be given to tutorial programs at the college level. Finally, this chapter will explore the use of peer tutorial methods with a "captive audience," students who attend school while in juvenile detention centers and other state-operated institutions.

218

PEER TUTORIAL PROGRAMS FOR UNMOTIVATED STUDENTS AND STATUS OFFENDERS

Faced with the task of providing educational programs to students who are "turned off" to education, concerned members of the juvenile justice system and the educational community have explored a number of alternatives to traditional classroom instruction. The reader may be familiar with the scope of the problem facing our communities: an increasing number of students are running away from home or from school. These youths may roam the streets for hours, days, or weeks, without any adult supervision, and definitely without any academic involvement. While there is little doubt that they are receiving an education, it hardly is of the sort that will help them to cope adequately with the intellectual demands of adult life. Working independently, the educational and the juvenile justice systems have attempted, first, to provide youth with alternatives to regular channels of educational involvement; and, second, to motivate these youths to take a more active role in obtaining an education.

A recent thrust in most academic circles has been towards career education, and in specialized instances, experience-based career education (EBCE). The thrust of career education is to provide students with current and valid information on the options available in various career fields. For example, students participating in career education activities may be given general information on several clusters of occupations that are available to potential employees. Students may delve in greater depth into the individual career cluster areas. In their exposure to careers, students become familiar with the entry requirements to jobs, including educational and training requirements, as well as with the monetary benefits of employment at particular jobs.

One focus in this area has been experience-based career education. Under such programs, students receive classroom instruction and guidance on career opportunities, and are given increasingly involved exposure to job sites and the role responsibilities inherent to those job sites. Several models of experience-based career education have been implemented nationally, sharing a common element of providing students with a sound basis of career information, career guidance, and career exploration. The federal government has made a commitment to implement EBCE programs nationwide, and to investigate the outcomes of such programs in relation to regular classroom programs.

Two innovative programs have focused on an underlying assumption of several EBCE models to provide tutorial services to their student population, status offenders. The underlying assumption utilized is that students can learn basic academic skills best when the materials used to teach these skills are individualized to approximate student competency levels and vocational needs. In other words, students who are provided with materials that are interesting and challenging are far more likely to learn these materials than they are those that are uninteresting and either below or above a student's skill level in task demand. In particular, one EBCE model stresses the importance of providing individualized instruction in the academic areas of reading, English, and math.

Importantly, EBCE programs that had previously been implemented, with few exceptions, served students who were either average or above average in intellectual ability. In many cases, such programs were available only to students at particular grade levels, i.e., usually junior or seniors in high school. The two programs described here were developed for students in grades six through twelve. These students with few exceptions either had run away from home in the past or had been absent from school so often that court procedures were initiated against them and their parents. Superficially, these students were considered to be status offenders by the juvenile justice system. The schools called them "non-attenders" or "school leavers" (the use of the word "dropout" usually is avoided because of its essentially negative connotations).

Program I

Created through the cooperative efforts of school and juvenile justice agencies, one project provided a wide range of activities for students. A day program included extensive opportunities for students to acquire academic credit in basic content areas. Material in these classes was individualized, and provided to students at their ability levels. The course content was not watered down but, rather, was designed to promote adult functional competency. Special care was given to the development of materials so that each student would satisfy the state requirements for the completion of credits to qualify for graduation from high school. It was very important to the high school students involved in the program to receive all possible credit towards graduation for their academic experiences.

Initial problems in working with status offenders were readily apparent. Program students often came to school with a defeatist attitude. Previous encounters with teachers and administrators had not been enjoyable or successful in terms of learning or receiving passing grades for courses. While this was not the only reason for their non-attendance, many of the students expressed belief that the traditional educational structure of the school system was insensitive to their emotional and cognitive needs. Stories of previous failure in a system that stressed the importance of everyone progressing at the same speed convinced program staff that individualized instruction and peer tutoring were two successful means of heightening student involvement in the learning process.

Introduced as an adjunct activity to individualized, teacher-directed instruction, peer tutoring was initially conceived as a method of furthering exposure to skill development for students. A staff of volunteer women was available initially to whom teachers could assign students judged to be in need of additional academic work. Little exposure to tutorial methods and strategies was given to these volunteers, but few people complained. The volunteers succeeded in building the involvement level of students in instructional activities. As such, these tutorial efforts fit in well with other program activities, which stressed the creation and maintenance of affective and cognitive involvement in the learning process. When project staff members realized that they could achieve more positive academic outcomes for learners by providing more structure to the tutorial process, changes were made in the tutorial component of the program. Adult volunteers were used only after a ten-hour training session on the content and techniques of the tutorial program. At this point, the staff implemented the use of volunteer "buddies" who served as friends and listeners to youths who sought such adult involvement. Volunteers in this role were trained in listening skills and communication techniques.

The outcome of the revised tutorial program was that students did learn tutorial content, and, thus, were better prepared to achieve in the classroom. Just as important an outcome was the enthusiasm that the students evidenced regarding the learning process. A concrete measure of the program's success was the increased attendance of students in the regular academic program. While the effects of the many program components cannot be separated, project staff firmly believed that the tutoring program contributed to the overall program's success.

During the second year of the program, staff teachers began to realize that their first-year students could make successful tutors. Selecting among students who volunteered for the role, teachers trained the tutor group in the responsibilities of the tutor role. A twenty-hour program covered such topics as the whys of tutoring, developing an atmosphere for learning, presenting materials in the correct sequence, and being sensitive to the learner's needs during the session. A group of ten tutors met with the first group of learning partners, students from the school who had signed up for extra academic instruction. From that group of students arose a group of seventy-five tutors who were on call to work with any other student in the school who requested short or long-term academic assistance. Several teachers in the school structured the involvement of tutors in their class, so that their students received assistance for definite periods with prespecified topics and skills. Students were actively involved in the development, under teacher supervision, of tutorial materials. Such was the success of the program that nearby elementary schools have called upon the program's tutors to work with their students.

Another result of the activities was a peer counselor program initiated by the school principal, who was interested in carrying the peer teaching concept one step further. Students were selected from a volunteer group to be trained in listening and communication skills. Peer counselors were expected to be expert listeners to their classmates. While not expected to solve the various emotional and/or affective problems of their peers, the counselors were able to help classmates sort out their thoughts and work towards solving conflicts. Problems discussed with the peer counselors would range from difficulties in studying to problems with dates. The peer counseling program has been well received by students and by staff. There has never been any reported difficulty in recruiting the counselors.

Program II

A different program for status offenders, one that works with a changing group of students at a variety of locations, resulted from the cooperation of a school system and the Juvenile Probation Department in a community. By definition, a truant is a student who is not attending school on a regular basis. Because the regular program of public education is offered in the daytime, some students choose to be truant so that they can work. In part a response to the working dropout, one school system began offering a tutorial program in basic English and math skills. The goal of the program was to increase the academic proficiencies of target students, and to promote successful return to either day or night school. An underlying attitude of many of the target students was that they might as well quit school because they were well behind their classmates in all skill areas. The tutorial program worked to undermine this attitude by creating a learning environment in which the students could succeed. Initial successes represented small steps in learning, but were followed by greater successes *and* changes in attitude. Students gradually became convinced that they could, with hard work, achieve the degree of educational training that they wanted to have. Counselors associated with the program assisted the students so that their expectations of the work required to complete their education were realistic. For example, a student who participated in the tutorial program would consult with the counselor when he was ready to change his involvement in the program. Students could choose to leave the tutorial program entirely and work, attend school, or some combination of the two. An option open to all students was to continue to receive tutoring while attending some other educational program.

Throughout the tenure of this program, its scope was significantly expanded. While continuing to work with the dropout, other students from ages ten to seventeen, who had decided to remain in school but continued to be excessively absent, were able to receive services offered by the program. Using an identical tutorial format, teachers worked during non-school hours to increase the English and math skills of their charges. A unique feature of this program was that the tutors were paid teachers. Training in tutorial methods and materials prepared the teachers for the sessions, but a large degree of the program's success stems from the "extras" that were added to their work. The teachers were instrumental in updating and improving both tutorial lesson content and the structure of the tutorial program. The teachers functioned as a team to evaluate program directions. As a result of the enthusiasm created by the staff, the program was expanded in its four years of existence to four times its original size.

Working meaningfully with the status offender to increase academic and social proficiency offers its own challenges to the educational community. Many educators have posited that the task is virtually impossible, while others proposed the use of highly budgeted "special schools" that effectively isolate such youths from their peers. The two programs described above fall somewhere in between these two extremes. While the first program worked with some status offenders, it also allowed for 25 percent of its students to be admitted with no labels attached. These students decided to enter the program in large part because of its career emphasis, a focus missing at other schools in the system. The selection committee for the program strove to achieve a mix of students, in terms of interests, backgrounds, and career goals. This method of creating a heterogeneous student body also enabled positive school behaviors to be modeled by the students. The second program described was much smaller in scope than the first program, but shared its commitment to provide its students educational experiences of quality. The tutorial method played a large role in the individualized academics of each program.

The experiences of the teachers and administrators of these programs provide us with clues for the effective use of instructional techniques with the status offender. The status offender, whether truant or a runaway, often is discouraged with the efficacy of traditional routes to receiving an education. Case studies of these youths reveal that many *perceived* little warmth or involvement with their teachers. Why such students became truants or runaways while similar classmates did not has been interpreted in a variety of ways, usually focusing on parental or other home-based antecedents. While it is not the authors' intent to delve into the reasons such students became status offenders, the implications of the content of students' perceptions is important. Assuming that they see themselves as distant from their teachers, with a resultant low level of achievement, the tutorial process may serve to reinvolve youths in school learning experiences.

To build involvement, the successful tutorial programs described above stressed the establishment of interest in actual learning early in the tutorial sessions. This was accomplished by taking time to introduce the tutorial program and to involve the learner in defining his or her goals for the sessions. Tutors in the programs had been trained in listening skills and became astute in drawing out the thoughts of the learners.

Once the learners had defined their goals for the tutorial sessions, the tutors helped their partners to state the goals *in writing*. One ongoing program developed a policy that learning goals would be incorporated in a standardized contract, that specifically would delineate the consequences of completing and not completing assignments. For some of the youths who had assigned caseworkers, contracts could involve outcomes that were applied by the parents. In one instance, an elaborate contract that involved goals for both learning and attendance provided one student with a "night on the town" with his parents. Besides motivating this particular student, the outcome encouraged family interaction. Other students worked very well for more traditional goals, including specific grades, the completion of assignments and a high school diploma. When the student was motivated to achieve a high school diploma, the attainment of such for work completion was a highly desired and readily demonstrable confirmation of progress towards a goal. The level of visibility of goal attainment, combined with the high level of teacher-student involvement, allows peer tutoring to be an effective tool with many status offenders. This has been shown to be so with both adult and peer student tutors. Perhaps the most satisfying outcomes for the staff members of programs with a status offender population are the changes in attitudes of the students toward school and teachers. More willing to pursue their educational goals, many of these students have successfully re-entered other, more advanced, educational programs and have proceeded to accomplish educational goals.

Few changes, if any, need be made in traditional content or structure of tutorial programs for these youths. Keeping in mind the principles of providing students with interesting materials presented in units small enough to digest, the educator can follow guidelines described earlier in this text to establish a tutorial program. The status offender shares with classmates the desire to contribute his or her input to the tutorial process, if given the chance. These students have been successfully involved as tutors themselves and as developers of tutorial materials in one program. Restricting the involvement of the status offender at any level of a tutorial program only serves to limit the potential outcomes that can be attained by these students. Because of this, tutorial programs for these students can follow the directions of programs provided for non-status offenders with similar learning needs.

ADULTS AS TUTORS

In the previous section, the tutors used in one program were paid adults. That these tutors were professional teachers added to the perceived effectiveness of their work with students. Up until this point, the term "peer tutoring" has been used to describe instances of children tutoring other children, usually at a close age or grade level. The studies and programs described in the historical perspectives section were of this type. However, there have been many tutorial programs that have worked with adult tutors, whether volunteers or paid for their services. This section will explore the adult as tutor and the advantages and disadvantages of such a person.

A previously cited example of the use of adult tutors occurs in Ellson et al.'s (1965) programmed tutoring studies. In several variations of the programmed approach, Ellson and his co-authors hired adult tutors to work with students in the tutorial sessions. Adults proceeded into their role as tutors after a training program, in which they became acquainted with the tutorial procedures used in the sessions.

Other peer tutorial programs have been able to exist only because of the availability of adult volunteer tutors. In an example of one such program, teachers in an elementary school approached their principal with the idea of starting a peer tutorial program using children teaching other children. While the principal agreed to the concept of students receiving tutorial assistance in subject areas, she did not think it feasible to have children tutoring other children. She stated that every child needed to devote all of his or her time to work in the classroom with teachers and aides. The principal did agree that adults could serve as tutors to the children, if interested adults could be located. By working through the school's Parent-Teacher Association, classroom teachers soon received an abundance of volunteer tutors. Volunteers included many women as well as several men. Following a brief orientation session in the tutorial process, the tutors received training in presentation of materials, feedback to students, and evaluation procedures. The tutorial program received the continuing support of the PTA, which contributed members' time to the organization of an after-school tutorial program to coincide with the school hours' program.

Another school system was fortunate in having a well-developed volunteers' program. Through a central office, adults in the community were recruited and trained for varying roles of working with children. A request for adult tutors from several schools was met by the office, which trained each participant for a tutorial program in reading and math. The adults were assigned to schools close to their homes, and individually contributed from two to ten hours a week as tutors. With the success of their tutor training program, the volunteer office undertook to train senior high students to serve as tutors in reading and math. These tutors then worked as volunteers in other high schools and at lower grade levels. The volunteer office was able, over a two-year period, to provide training for tutors in thirty schools.

The two systems described above are similar to many programs across the nation which have flourished with the assistance of adult volunteer tutors. School systems may not have considered the option of having children tutoring other children. Indeed, often it is believed that adults are the only possible tutors. While there has been little research which has compared use of adult versus peer tutors, the earlier mentioned study of Thomas (1970) should be remembered. In his work, Thomas discovered that child (peer) tutors were as effective as college education majors in producing reading gains following tutoring with second graders. Additionally, the child tutors were more direct and businesslike with their partners, less willing to resort to coaxing and games. Adults, however, are a feasible alternative to the use of child tutors for several reasons. First, as may have occurred to the reader from an earlier example, children in the classroom who could serve as tutors may need to devote themselves to their own learning. The demands on a student's time include daily lessons and preparing for future activities, including tests. Adults who are able to volunteer for tutorial programs are usually able to devote a specified amount of time over a definite period. Secondly, adults can become available more readily before, during, and after school for tutoring. After all, the adults have to answer primarily to themselves, while the children have to deal with their parents.

The issue of pay for tutoring services may influence the choice of adult versus child tutors. The literature on tutoring has indicated that most paid tutors fall into the adult category. There have been several federally supported programs, primarily those directed to the support of low income students, which have recruited and paid teenagers as tutors. More common is the instance of a school district that provided compensation at minimum wage standards to adult tutors. Money may be a deciding factor in certain areas in recruiting a sufficient number of tutors to support a program. With adults, however, and working through established channels with parent groups (PTA, PTO, etc.), there should be little difficulty in obtaining an abundance of tutors.

TUTORS AT THE COLLEGE LEVEL

Although little attention will be devoted here to tutoring at the college level, the reader should be aware that it is a common occurrence. As any college student can attest, paid tutors can be found on every campus in the country, or at least in every college town. Departments in many universities have organized programs to tutor students in particular course work. Very few of these departments train tutors for their role. Rather, tutors are often graduate students who receive a stipend for their activities.

Schools of education attached to universities usually make available to local school districts a number of services for area school students. Several examples exist of tutorial services being offered to individuals and to small groups of students. On several occasions contained in earlier references, local communities have benefited from large-scale tutorial programs conducted under the supervision of area universities.

A college tutorial program that did succeed in its goals occurred on one campus. Created to attract children of migrant workers to the college campus, this program toured the state of Texas meeting and discussing its activities with target youth. Once the student enrolled on campus, the program's staff focused on providing peer counseling and orientation to college life. Peer counselors generally were students who had been previously involved in the program. When classes started, the students received individual and small-group counseling in their course work from paid peer tutors, including students previously involved in the program. The program worked intensively with students during their first year on campus, and was successful in helping program youths to pass the majority of their courses. With peer tutoring and peer counseling combined, the program was successful in guiding students to remain in college, even if it was not the one they attended during their freshman year.

The success of this program inspired other educators in the community to work with high school-age students who had migrant worker parents. Because of the nature of migrant work and the income associated with it, many migrant youths had not considered the possibility of attending college. Through a variety of funding sources, a program for orientation to college life and academics was implemented, using college-aged couselors as youth organizers. High school youths who indicated an interest in attending college were given an extended orientation to college life and could receive, if they desired, tutoring from the counselors in high school subjects. The orientation and tutoring activities lessened the anxiety of the students about to attend college.

In describing the process of instituting and evaluating tutorial programs, the authors have stressed the importance of working closely with school administrators and parents of students in target schools. When a university-supported tutorial project is proposed for a school or series of schools, the process of meeting the needs of administrators and parents is similarly important. Many school districts across the nation have well-defined standards and procedures by which universities can become involved in research activities. A common strategy in school districts is for the research plan to be approved by district administrative staff and to have *all* parents of involved students sign a form agreeing to the project activities.

PEER TUTORING IN INSTITUTIONAL SETTINGS

In an earlier chapter, several studies are described in which children in institutional settings received peer tutoring services. Although the tutoring programs discussed were those that occurred in institutions for the mentally retarded, there have been applications of the peer tutoring model in settings for the mentally disturbed, hospital patients, and the incarcerated. The use of peers as therapeutic change agents has been documented by Prentice and Sperry (1965) and more recently by McGee, Kauffman and Nussen (1977). Without delving deeply into the research components of such tutoring programs, representative programs will be described in detail.

Wagner and Sternlicht (1975) reported success at an institution for the mentally retarded in which retarded adolescents were successful in a tutoring program with retarded children. During the study (described in greater detail in the last chapter), adolescent residents (mean IQ 34) at the institution were trained for thirty hours in the art of teaching dressing skills. Working with a group of younger children who served as trainees, the tutors devoted three weeks to teaching dressing skills to their partners. Following the first phase of the program, tutors were trained in an eating skills component for thirty hours. Trainees received twenty hours of involvement with peers in the eating skills portion of the program. Outcomes of the program were that the trainees made positive changes in dressing and in eating skills. The program was judged a success by program administrators.

A program with a similar population at a state institution for the mentally retarded attempted a program in which students with higher intelligence and social adjustment levels worked with less able peers in mastering basic math and reading materials. Although no formal evaluation was made of outcomes, a staff participant noted that students enjoyed working with each other and seemed to concentrate on their tasks as well as they had with an adult instructor. Clearly, there is an abundance of opportunities for use of peer assistance activites with the retarded institutionalized citizen. Peer-aided activities could include tutoring as described above, peer counseling at the "buddy" level, and small group peer problem-solving. Training of tutors should be intensive and complete to prepare the tutors for the frustrations inherent in the tutorial sessions. Attention to the social abilities and tolerance levels of selected tutors is advised.

Similar considerations would apply to the use of residents in institutions for the mentally/behaviorally disturbed. In many such institutions, the use of peer counselors has been ongoing for several years. Many such programs support an educational component or work in close conjunction with nearby school programs to meet the academic needs of their clients. In an educational environment, peer tutoring activities are a logical extension of the classroom process. With the wide range of ages to be found in many institutions for the retarded and the disturbed, the term "peer" may imply that the tutorial partners are at a similar status, not age. In one state-supported institution, clients in the educational component were recruited and trained to serve as peer tutors, after staff reviewed the aggressiveness and coping abilities of the residents with their peers. The students were given the option of participating in the tutorial program. Few refused the opportunity. The overwhelming reactions of staff, tutors, and their partners were positive. The tutors freed the teacher to devote more time to students with more serious academic or emotional needs.

A wilderness residential program for emotionally disturbed children provided peer tutorial support to many of the children in the academic component delivered at the base camp. Reports of the tutoring's success in creating a positive learning atmosphere for tutor and learner have encouraged program staff to involve more students in such activities.

A child who is receiving long-term care at home or in a hospital setting qualifies in many areas to receive tutoring at the bed site. Tutors are usually paid members of the public or private school system, who attempt to provide academic activities for the child that will allow that child to keep pace with classmates in their learning. When the reasons for bed care involve disease, tutorial involvement has been exclusively with the paid adult tutor. When the child is confined with an injury, there have been a few efforts to involve peers as tutors. Of course, under the circumstances, peers are a welcome sight to the bedridden child. One school made an announcement over its intercom requesting classmates of an injured boy to visit him at home while he recovered from an automobile accident. The interest of the classmates was so high that the child's parents were overwhelmed by visitors. One teacher, recognizing the concern of the students and their interest in helping their classmate as much as possible, arranged for a different classmate in each subject area to tutor the boy at home. The tutoring allowed the child to keep pace with peers and to make the best of an admittedly bad situation. The boy finally was able to leave his bed and return to school. Although he was somewhat behind in certain classes, his peers continued to provide tutoring until he had caught up with the group.

Adolescents or adults incarcerated for more than a few days are able to receive educational or vocational training at the institution in which they are placed. For the adult prisoner, these training activities occur in state and federal institutions for convicted prisoners. Teachers are paid members of the general staff and are involved in overall supervision of the inmates. Volunteers from the community and prisoners are occasionally trained to serve as classroom aides and tutors. Tutoring with an exclusively adult population will not be discussed here.

Involvement in educational activities occurs much sooner after the arrest and detention process with the adolescent. In one Texas county detention center for adolescents, educational and craft activities begin on the second day of a youth's incarceration. The activities continue until the youth's dismissal from the center. As in the case of other institutions, some adolescent detention centers provide their own educational services while others contract with area school districts for teachers and material services. The adolescent who is adjudicated by the courts and assigned to a long-term form of incarceration usually begins educational and vocational training activities soon after placement. Teaching at these settings is usually under close supervision. Teacher/student ratios are very low. Indeed, in one drug-related offenses program, staff outnumbered students by three to one. With the ready availability of adults and the unwillingness of administrators to surrender total supervision of their charges, few opportunities may exist for peer tutoring by peers.

An exception to this occurred in one center for incarcerated youth. Many dollars had been given to staff to purchase educational materials. Outside consultants had visited the staff and trained them in the use of new and innovative instructional strategies. The teachers were able to enforce classroom standards of behavior with restrictions on students' freedom outside of the class. With all of this going for them, teachers found that they had to devote a great deal of energy and time to motivating students to learn. One staff member decided to train two of his students to tutor students who were extremely poor readers in his class. Tutorial sessions were not very structured but did occur under the supervision of the teacher. With tutoring, students in the reading class became for the first time excited about their daily meetings. Classroom disruptions went to zero, while other teachers' interest in the reading teacher's activities skyrocketed. Soon the reading teacher was helping his colleagues to develop tutoring programs with students throughout the school. These teachers found student interest in academics to increase with the infusion of tutoring into the regular academic program. A variation of the tutoring program that also produced positive outcomes was for new students in the program to receive the majority of their initial academic training from peer tutors. Entering students, under this arrangement, quickly became adjusted to the total academic program at the institution.

This chapter has outlined several variations in peer tutoring services. The use of the adult tutor, whether paid or unpaid, has been a common sight in many schools. The application of peer tutoring to specialized settings has been much less common, although innovative programs have met or exceeded their expectations of success. The message that peer tutoring *can* be a positive force in educating almost all children is intended to inspire the reader to adapt peer tutoring in new and exciting ways. The reader who attempts to meet the challenge of educating children in specialized learning environments can successfully use peer tutoring by following the guidelines for adaptation detailed in earlier chapters.

REFERENCES

Argyle, M. Social skills theory. In V.L. Allen (Ed.), *Children as teachers.* New York: Academic Press, 1976.

Bateson, G. *Steps to an ecology of mind.* New York: Ballantine, 1972.

Bell, A. *Bell's mutual tuition and moral discipline.* London: C.J.G. and F. Livingston, 1832. Reference in Gartner, Kohler, and Riessman, 1971.

Bell, S.E., Garlock, N.L., and Colella, S.L. Students as tutors: High schoolers and elementary pupils. *Clearing House,* 1969, *44,* 242–244.

Bouchillon, P., and Bouchillon, B. Students learn by tutoring. *Contemporary Education,* 1972, *43,* 281–283.

Brown, L., Fenrick, N., and Klemme, H. Trainable pupils learn to teach each other. *Teaching Exceptional Children,* 1971, *4,* 18–24.

Cartwright, C.A., and Cartwright, G.P. *Developing observational skills.* New York: McGraw-Hill, 1974.

Cicirelli, V.G. Siblings teaching siblings. In V.L. Allen (Ed.), *Children as teachers.* New York: Academic Press, 1976.

Cloward, R.D. Studies in tutoring. *Journal of Experimental Education,* 1967, *36* (1), 14–25.

Cohen, A.D., Kirk, J.C., and Dickson, W.P. *Guidebook for tutors with an emphasis on tutoring minority children.* Stanford: Stanford University, Committee on Linguistics, 1972. (ERIC Document Reproduction No. ED. 084-326).

Collins, J.F., and Calevro, M.J. *Mainstreaming special education using a peer tutoring system and a minimum objective curriculum for nine eighth grade students.* May, 1974. (ERIC Document Reproduction No. 102-788).

Dahlen, G.G. *The effect of like ethnic qualities upon reading tutoring of third graders.* U.S. Dept. of H.E.W. 1973 (ERIC Document Reproduction No. ED 095-488).

Deterline, W.C. *Training and management of student-tutors. Final Report.* Palo Alto, Calif.: General Programmed Teaching, 1970. (ERIC Document Reproduction No. ED 048-133).

Ehly, S. *Experimental Analysis of Tutor, Tutee, and Process Variables in tutorial learning.* Unpublished Doctoral Dissertation, University of Texas, Austin, 1975.

Ehly, S. Peer tutorial models. Paper presented at the 55th Annual Convention of the Council for Exceptional Children (Atlanta, April, 1977).

Ehly, S.W., and Larsen, S.C. Tutor and tutee characteristics as predictors of tutorial outcomes. *Psychology in the Schools,* 1976, *8,* 348-349.

Ellson, D.G., Barber, L. Engle, T.L., and Kampwerth, L. Programmed tutoring: a teaching aid and a research tool. *Reading Research Quarterly,* 1965, *1* (1).

Ellson, D.G., Harris, P., and Barber, L. A field test of programmed and directed tutoring. *Reading Research Quarterly,* 1968, *3* (3).

Engel, R.C. Trainable students as tutors. *The Pointer,* 1974, *19,* 131.

Etters, E.M. Tutorial assistance in college core courses. *Journal of Educational Research,* 1967, *60,* 406-407.

Evans, C.M., and Potter, R.E. The effectiveness of the S-pack when administered by sixth-grade children to primary grade children. *Language, Speech, and Hearing Services in Schools,* 1974, *5* (2), 85-90.

Fleming, J.C. Pupil tutors and tutees learn together. *Today's Education,* 1969, *58* (7), 22-24.

Forlan, G., and Wrightstone, J.W. Measuring the quality of social acceptability within a class. *Educational and Psychological Measurement,* 1955, *15,* 127-136.

Fowle, W.B. *The teachers' institute.* New York: A.S. Barnes, 1866. Reference in Gartner, Kohler, and Riessman, 1971.

Galvin, J., and Shoup, M.L. The use of peers in teaching reading to withdrawn children. Reference in Gartner, Kohler, and Riessman, 1971.

Gartner, A., Kohler, M.C., and Riessman, F. *Children teach children—Learning by teaching.* New York: Harper & Row, 1971.

Geiser, R.L. Some of our worst students teach! *Catholic School Journal*, 1969, *69* (6), 18-20.

Gordon, I.J. *Studying the child in school.* New York: John Wiley & Sons, 1966.

Hagen, J.W., and Moeller, T. *Cross-age tutoring.* Ann Arbor, Michigan: Michigan University, Department of Psychology, July, 1971. (ERIC Document Reproduction No. ED 085-090).

Hall, R.V. *Managing behavior.* Lawrence, Kan.: H & H Enterprises, 1971.

Hamblin, J.A., and Hamblin, R.L. On teaching disadvantaged preschoolers to read: A successful experiment. *American Educational Research Journal.* 1972, *9*, 209-216.

Harrington, J. Peer teaching. *The Pointer*, 1974, *19*, (3).

Harrison, G.V. *Dissertation Abstracts*, 1969, University of California at Los Angeles. Reference in Deterline, 1970.

Hassinger, J., and Via, M. How much does a tutor learn through teaching reading? *Journal of Secondary Education*, 1969, *44*, 42-44.

Horan, J.J., deGirolomo, M.A., Hill, R.L., and Shute, R.E. The effects of older — peer participant models on deficient academic performance. *Psychology in the Schools*, 1974, *11*, 207-211.

Johnson, H. Pupils are teachers: A brief survey of current programs. *Social Policy*, 1970, *1* (4), 69-71.

Klaus, D.J. *Patterns of peer tutoring.* Paper presented at the Annual Meeting of the American Education Research Association. (Washington, D.C., March, 1975). (ERIC Document Reproduction No. ED 103-356).

Lancaster, J. *Improvements in education.* London: Collins and Perkins, 1806. Reference in Gartner, Kohler, and Riessman, 1971.

Landrum, J.W., and Martin, M.D. When students teach others. *Educational Leadership*, 1970, *27*, 446-448.

Lederman, M.J. The metamorphosis: Dreams he found himself transformed into an English teacher. New York: C.U.N.Y., 1974. (ERIC Document Reproduction No. ED 091-706).

Lewis, W.A., Lovell, J.T., and Jessee, B.E. Interpersonal relationships and pupil progress. *Personnel and Guidance Journal*, 1965, *44*, 396-401.

Lippitt, P., and Lohman, J.E. Cross-age relationships—an educational resource. *Children*, 1965, *12*, 113-117.

Little, D.F., and Walker, B.S. Tutor-pupil relationship and academic progress. *Personnel and Guidance Journal*, 1968, *47*, 324-328.

McGee, C.S., Kauffman, J.M., and Nussen, J.L. Children as therapeutic change agents: Reinforcement intervention paradigms. *Review of Educational Research*, 1977, *47*, 451-477.

McWhorter, K.T., and Levy, J. The influence of a tutorial program upon tutors. *Journal of Reading*, 1970, *14*, 221-224.

Newmark, G., and Melaragno, R.J. *Tutorial community project: Report on the first year, May, 1968–June, 1969.* Santa Monica, California: Systems Development Corporation, 1969.

Oakland, T., and Williams, F.C. An evaluation of two methods of peer tutoring. *Psychology in the Schools*, 1975, *12*, 166-171.

Prentice, N.M., and Sperry, B.M. Therapeutically oriented tutoring of children with primary neurotic learning inhibitions. *American Journal of Orthopsychiatry*, 1965, *35*, 521-530.

Rosenbaum, P.S. *Peer-mediated instruction.* New York: Teachers College Press, 1973.

Ross, S.F. *A study to determine the effects of peer tutoring on the reading efficiency and self concept of disadvantaged community college freshmen: A final report.* Fort Worth, Texas: Tarrant County College District, 1972. (ERIC Document Reproduction No. ED 081-415).

Rowell, C.G. A prototype for an individualized spelling program. *Elementary English*, 1972, *49*, 335-340.

Snapp, M. *A study of the effects of tutoring by fifth and sixth graders on the reading achievement scores of first, second, and third graders.* Unpublished doctoral dissertation, University of Texas, Austin, 1970.

Snapp, M., Oakland, T., and Williams, F.C. A study of individualizing instruction by using elementary school children as tutors. *Journal of School Psychology*, 1972, *10*, 1-8.

Snipes, W.C. An inquiry: Peer group teaching in freshman writing. *College Composition and Communication*, 1971, *22*, 169-174.

Strain, P.S., Cooke, T.P., and Apolloni, T. The role of peers in modifying classmates' social behavior: A review. *Journal of Special Education*, 1976a, *10*, 351-356.

Strain, P.S., Cooke, T.P., and Apolloni, T. *Teaching Exceptional Children.* New York: Academic Press, 1976b.

Thomas, J.L. *Tutoring strategies and effectiveness: A comparison of elementary age tutors and college age tutors.* Unpublished doctoral dissertation, University of Texas, Austin, 1970.

Tillett, W.S., Porter, D.H., and Joiner, S.E. *The peer teaching program of community college studies.* Miami, Florida: Miami-Dade Junior College, March, 1972. (ERIC Document Reproduction No. ED 060-837).

Vassallo, W. Learning by tutoring. *American Education*, 1973, *9* (3), 25-28.

Wagner, P., and Sternlicht, M. Retarded persons as "teachers":

Retarded adolescents tutoring retarded children. *American Journal of Mental Deficiency*, 1975, *79*, 674-679.

White, J. Programmed tutor. *American Education*, 1971, *7*, 18-21.

Yuthas, L.J. Student tutors in a college remedial program. *Journal of Reading*, 1970, *14*, 231-234.

INDEX